A Sight of the Saviour

Beholding Jesus in John 11

Richard Brooks

EP BOOKS

(Evangelical Press) Unit C, Tomlinson Road, Leyland, England, PR25 2DY

www.epbooks.org
epbooks@10ofthose.com

First published 2022

British Library Cataloguing in Publication Data available

ISBN: 978-1-78397-318-7

Designed by Jude May

Cover image © Fritz Jorgensen | iStock, KatyaKatya | Adobe Stock

Contents

To begin with

We talk about visiting different places in order to see the sights. When we visit the Bible, God's own word, there are endless sights to see. They are wonderful sights, breathtaking sights. They are sights which, once seen, remain with you forever. They become sights which you wish to see again and again. They are sights where you see and appreciate more every time you visit them.

By far the most exquisite sights to be found in the Bible are the many sights of the Lord Jesus Christ. This should not surprise us, for when speaking of the Scriptures Jesus himself declares, 'it is they that bear witness about me' (John 5:39). Within these pages, from their opening page to their closing page, Jesus is revealed to us. You cannot miss him. In particular, they tell us about his person (who he is) and his work (what he has done, is doing, and will do). And they reveal so much to us about what it means for us to belong to him by faith.

This book aims to explore this from just one chapter, chapter 11 of John's gospel. In 20:31 of this gospel, the apostle John tells us why he wrote. He did so, he says to all who read it, 'so that you may believe that Jesus is the Christ, the Son of God, and that by believing you may have life in his name'.

Why John 11? Because this single chapter of 57 verses shows us one glorious thing after another concerning Jesus. While there is much more that could be said about him than this chapter contains, it is remarkably comprehensive. Would you know Jesus? Or, if you know him already, would you know him better? Then John 11 is a very fruitful place for you to look.

I have called this book *A Sight of the Saviour*. It focusses upon 19 different things about him. The book's subtitle is *Beholding Jesus in John 11*. That word 'beholding' is carefully chosen. The basic meaning of the verb is 'to see' or 'to observe', but there is more to it than that. It can carry the sense of wonder, amazement, even pleasure. The chapter records an astounding miracle: Jesus raises from his tomb a man who has been dead for four days. It is a very moving narrative, involving a family of a brother and two sisters, three people who were among Jesus' most precious friends during his time on earth. So much of human life and experience (including yours and mine) is here.

Several centuries ago a man prayed a prayer concerning himself and the Lord Jesus Christ which expressed his desire to know Jesus more clearly, to love Jesus more dearly, and to follow Jesus more nearly. May that be our mutual desire as we set off together now.

The Bible version I am using is the English Standard Version (ESV).

1

Jesus' matchless love

John 11:1–4

There is only one place for our sight of the Saviour to begin, and that is exactly where this chapter of John's gospel begins—with the matchless love of Jesus. There are two aspects to *Jesus' matchless love* which need to take our attention: *what it is* and *what it does.*

The love of Jesus: what it is

What kind of a love is the love of Jesus? What is it like? How would you describe it? We sing of 'the deep, deep love of Jesus' and affirm that 'The love of Jesus, what it is, none but his loved ones know.'

If you speak to an unbeliever about the love of Jesus you will likely get no response. The reason for that is that the only ones who know anything about it are his loved ones: those who are actually loved by Jesus and know it, those who have experienced his love in a personal way, who delight in it and are immensely thankful for it, those who adore him on account of it. Even then, there is so very much more of his love still to be known and relished. The apostle Paul acknowledged this for himself and for every Christian. For the Christians in the church at Ephesus, this was his heartfelt prayer: 'that Christ may dwell in your hearts through faith—that you, being rooted and grounded in love, may have strength to comprehend with all the saints what is the breadth and length and height and depth, and to know the love of Christ that surpasses knowledge' (Ephesians 3:17–19). The Ephesians were already Christians. They already knew the love of Christ, but there was still so much more. Oh that we can all say, to the glory of God, 'Jesus loves me, this I know'.

The scene, as John chapter 11 opens, is Bethany, a village located some two miles from Jerusalem at the Mount of Olives, a lovely place of fig trees, almonds and pomegranates. However, its chief attraction and affection in Jesus' eyes lay in the fact that living there were three people whom he loved and who loved him. It was a home of three dear souls whose names were written in heaven, two sisters and a brother. We are introduced to them straightaway in the opening verse: Lazarus and his sisters Mary and Martha. They have been described as 'going hand in hand to glory'.

Yet there was a dark shadow hanging over that dear home and those dear hearts. 'Now a certain man was ill, Lazarus of Bethany'. The brother in the family was a sick man and his sisters were greatly concerned for him. So what did they do? They sent a message to Jesus to tell him and to seek his aid. The message could scarcely have been briefer or more to the point, and while it states that Lazarus was ill (and the implication, surely, is that he was very ill and that their desire was that Jesus would come and make him well), all it said was this: 'Lord, [literally, 'Lord, behold' or 'Lord, look'] he whom you love is ill'. That is all. Not 'he who loves you', not that way round. Just, 'he whom you love' or 'the one you love'. No name mentioned. That was Mary and Martha's plea for Lazarus, that Jesus loves him! That was all they needed to say. Yet how deeply they spoke from their hearts to Jesus' heart! Addressing Jesus as 'Lord', in the way that they did, was their humbling of themselves before his deity and power. They made no demand. They let Jesus know and left the matter with him. They trusted him and they waited for him. They deemed that sufficient.

What, then, is the love of Jesus? In its widest scriptural sense, it is *the love of an eternal Saviour*. Jesus had loved Lazarus from 'before the foundation of the world' (Ephesians 1:4). And he has loved and does love all of his own with this eternal, everlasting love. We call it an *electing* love, for God chose to love us (electing meaning choosing); a *pardoning* love, for 'while we were still sinners, Christ died for us' (Romans 5:8); a *sacrificial* love, for it took him all the way to the cross, to Calvary; and a *drawing* love, as he makes us willing in the day of his power, so that now 'We love (him) because he first loved us' (1 John 4:19). But it is something else as well, which arises directly from the account here in John 11: it is a *personal* love. Notice again the 'he' of verse 3, with no mention at all of Lazarus' name. To which Jesus does not send the messenger back to ask, 'who is he? Who do you mean?' No. A word from the sisters saying 'he' says it all to Jesus. How so? 'The Lord knows those who are his' (2 Timothy 2:19).

Furthermore, the love of Jesus is *the love of a faithful friend*. He is a friend who 'loves at all times' (Proverbs 17:17) and 'who sticks closer than a brother' (Proverbs 18:24). This unique friendship is the love of a *concerned* friend, an *upholding* friend, a *sustaining* friend, a *forgiving* friend, a *providing* friend, a *dependable* friend, an *unchanging* friend and, most significantly of all, a *loving* and *faithful* friend.

This is the love with which the Lord Jesus Christ loved Lazarus and Mary and Martha. It was the love of an eternal Saviour and a faithful friend. And this is exactly the same love which he has for all his own. There is no love like the love of Jesus, nothing to match it or to compare with it. And there is no experience like being the object of his care and affection, nothing to match or compare with that either. The three siblings at Bethany rejoiced in the assurance of it. Do we? Do you? They knew 'the love of Jesus, what it is', and so the sisters sent this simple, heartfelt message to Jesus. How important it is to possess a deep, precious and blessed assurance in your very soul that you are loved by Jesus, that you are one of his own loved ones. Is he your eternal Saviour? Is he your faithful friend?

The love of Jesus: what it does

What effect should the clear knowledge and experience of Jesus' love have upon us? What should it 'do' to us? What difference should it make? What do we learn from the Bethany home?

First, *the love of Jesus does not exempt the believer from sickness, trial and affliction*. 'Lord, he whom you *love* is *ill*.' The love of Jesus does not separate us from the common infirmities of life. Christians have bodies, like everyone else, and so are subject to all manner of illness, trial and affliction like everyone else and, if anything, more so. How, more so? Because of the disciplining, chastening (though always loving) hand of our gracious God (on the one hand), and—very differently—because of the malice of our great enemy, the devil (on the other).

Jesus, as is clear, had a very special love for Lazarus, and this will become even more apparent as this chapter of John's gospel unfolds. Yet he was seriously ill (the sisters would surely not have sent this message to Jesus if they did not judge the matter urgent). Maybe they were concerned even for their brother's life. So what must we learn if we are Christians? That we must never for one moment start doubting the love of Jesus towards us whenever he appears to be laying a heavy hand upon us. Just as a surgeon, when operating on a patient, looks and focuses with particular care upon his patient, so the Lord Jesus Christ (the divine physician) is demonstrating his love even more (not less!) when in one way or another his own ones, whom he loves, are up against it. Not less, more! The matter may even be stated as boldly as this: the one whom the Lord loves is in a far better condition when he is sick or tried, than is the unbeliever when he is in full health and vigour.

Second, *the love of Jesus gives us a holy boldness when we approach him.* Here is 'mercy and ... grace to help in time of need' (Hebrews 4:16). Timely grace and mercy awaits us at the throne of heavenly grace. To him we may bring all our burdens, all our sorrows, all our sins and all our cares, remembering that our eternal Saviour and faithful Friend is there in heaven as our great high priest, always bearing our names upon his heart.

Mary and Martha would not have considered even for one moment that this was something in which Jesus would not be interested or that he would not wish to be bothered with. They would not have regarded their messenger as being on a fruitless errand. No! By no means! Lazarus, whom Jesus loved, was poorly. They did not imagine that this was a case too small (or too large) for Jesus' attention. They wrote delicately but passionately as they made known their request to Jesus.

How much we too need to discover (or, perhaps, rediscover) that we *cannot* have true peace in any condition or circumstance until we tell the Lord about it, until we bring it to the Lord in prayer. And, just as much, how we also need to discover (or, perhaps, rediscover) that we *need not* have anxiety in any condition or circumstance once we *have* told the Lord about it.

Moreover, Mary and Martha not only sought Jesus in the matter, but actually *believed*. In contrast, our problem can sometimes be that not only do we 'not have, because [we] do not ask' (James 4:2), but that even when we do ask, we do not necessarily believe. We have to plead with the unnamed father in the gospels, 'I believe; help my unbelief!' (Mark 9:24). When all the time the love of Jesus bids us come, ask and welcome—every time!

Third, *the love of Jesus provides us with one after another of God's great and precious promises*. Verse 4 records Jesus' response upon receipt of the message (and the messenger, no doubt, would have relayed this message back to the Bethany home where the sisters would have eagerly been awaiting news). Jesus' response was this: 'This illness does not lead to death.' How relieved and thankful Mary and Martha would have been to hear those words. Surely they came as an immediate answer not only to their message but (more importantly) to their prayers. How their anxious faces and beating hearts must have been calmed, quieted and soothed. And there was more in the message, of course. Not only would Lazarus' illness 'not lead to death', but this also: 'It is for the glory of God, so that the Son of God may be glorified through it.' A lot was to happen, however, before all became plain.

2

Jesus' perfect timing

John 11:4–6

Something puzzling awaits here, at first sight. The Bethany sisters, Mary and Martha, have sent an urgent message to Jesus, stating the matter very compactly, without a word wasted. 'Lord, he whom you love is ill.' The Lord Jesus lost no time in sending his reply via the messenger who had been sent to him: 'This illness does not lead to death.' What blessing and comfort those few words must have brought to the anxious home. But there then follows what might have struck Mary and Martha (and perhaps strikes us, who read about it) as puzzling. They (and we) might imagine that almost the very moment that Jesus heard of his friend Lazarus' illness and the concern of his sisters for him, he would (we say it reverently) have dropped everything he was doing, *not only* sending the encouraging news with which verse 4 begins, *but also* hastening to Bethany as soon as possible in order to minister to the precious family. Especially in the light of what is so beautifully stated in verse 5: 'Now Jesus loved Martha and her sister and Lazarus.' That is not, however, what happened.

'So, when he heard that Lazarus was ill, he stayed two days longer in the place where he was' (verse 6). No prompt rushing to Bethany. No sudden appearance at their door. Rather, it was Jesus' hearing of the sickness which led him, quite deliberately and knowing exactly what he was doing, to stay put where he was for two whole days. It appears, upon the face of it, to be a most extraordinary, unexpected and unnecessary delay. But no! What it actually demonstrates is *Jesus' perfect timing*.

The divine timing, in all things, is always absolutely perfect. 'This God—his way is perfect' (Psalm 18:30). And Jesus, always remember, is God. The Lord is not like the transport services: sometimes late, sometimes early, sometimes on time. He is never late and never early, but always right on time, the time which he appoints. And the better we grasp this, the richer our Christian life and experience will be. On the other hand, the poorer our grasp upon this great and fundamental truth about the divine ways, then the more trouble we shall be letting ourselves in for.

So the question we face from this section of John 11 is precisely this: why did Jesus delay? When Mary and Martha were in this extremity, and when we are in the same or a similar position, calling upon him and seeking his face in prayer, as we are bidden to do—why does the Lord sometimes *appear* to delay, take his time, keep us waiting? In the present instance, why did Jesus stay 'two days longer' where he was, while still assuring the sisters that he loved them? The connection between Jesus 'loved' and Jesus 'stayed' seems strange, but was for several reasons, each of which is worth exploring a little and each of which is bound up with the others.

It was a delay of glory

That is to say, as Jesus himself says, 'It is for the glory of God, so that the Son of God may be glorified through it' (verse 5). This is without doubt the one overriding and all-surpassing reason for the delay, and so must be considered first. It clearly stands out in Jesus' mind, purpose and intention. It towers over everything else.

It is all too easy, sadly, to become hemmed in by our own circumstances. We ask (even if only to ourselves, and without uttering any words) questions like these: How long is this trial, sickness, or whatever it is, going to last? Why hasn't this prayer been answered yet? How long am I going to have to wait? What possible good can come out of all this delaying? Yet in all these questions we put ourselves at the centre. What thought is to be found there of concern for the glory of God? What evidence of a patient waiting upon God, until he acts for his own glory? What expectancy of what remarkable things the Lord might do in his own perfect time?

Maybe thoughts such as these were going through the minds of Mary and Martha as the hours passed and they waited, with still no sign of Jesus arriving. We can only speculate (although hints will be provided later in verses 21 and 32). Yet there was a vital lesson for them in all of this apparent delay, just as there is for the rest of us who, like them, belong to the Saviour.

God is God. So God is glorious. The Father is glorious, the Son is glorious, the Spirit is glorious. And just as all that God *is* is a demonstration of his glory, so all that he *does* demonstrates his glory too. When he acts and when he holds back. When he gives, and when he denies. When his dealings are plain and clear and when they appear puzzling and perplexing. It is all for his glory. And that is what it was here in the episode before us: Lazarus' sickness, Jesus staying put for two days, and (still to come) Lazarus dying and his sisters' consequent grief. Every part of it was 'for the glory of God, so that the Son of God may be glorified through it'. It is the chief end of all the divine purposes.

How, then, is his glory seen here?

It was a delay of wisdom

In no way was Jesus playing some cruel game with the Bethany women. There are no divine games, ever. 'The LORD reigns' (Psalm 97:1), and this reigning triune God is altogether wise. This attribute comes through plentifully in Scripture. Two examples must suffice in order to establish the point. 'With God are wisdom and might; he has counsel and understanding' (Job 12:13); '… to the only wise God be glory for evermore through Jesus Christ' (Romans 16:27).

The point of this in the present context is that all the time, Jesus knew what he was doing. He knew why he delayed, even if Mary and Martha did not. In particular, he was doing three things in his wisdom.

First, *he was reminding them who he is:* he is God. This great truth is always central and fundamental in Scripture, and needs continually to be learned and re-learned by the children of God. He was desiring to show them that he knew the end from the beginning and that he was in complete knowledge and control of all the little family's circumstances. As a result, even the delay—especially the delay—was wisely appointed. They would come to see that soon enough and with great blessing.

Second, *he was strengthening and increasing their faith and dependence.* And he was doing this in multiple ways, that they might know and enjoy more than they had ever done before the might of his arm, the warmth of his embrace, the sweetness of his love, the tenderness of his voice, the shelter of his wings, the wisdom of his designs and the perfection of all his ways. For them and for us, these things are not learned in a moment. For them and for us, these things are not learned without trials and afflictions. Spiritual graces such as faith, dependence, contentment, patience, perseverance and godly fear are among those graces which (as has often been observed) grow best in winter. There are no experiences like waiting upon the Lord in our trials and his apparent 'delays' to teach us these things, and to teach us them well. They so often lead to Christian maturity in some of its choicest blooms.

Third, *he was directing them to believe and lean upon his promises.* This shines out here. Jesus' words to them in verse 4 were words of pure promise. Consider them again. 'This illness does not lead to death.' Surely that is plain enough. True, Lazarus was going to die, but that was far from being the end of what happened, as we shall discover, and so did the two women! Jesus was looking further than death itself. Our God is the maker, keeper and performer of promises. He is indeed the promising God. And from one perspective, the entire Bible is a casket of his promises. Search them out for yourself, knowing assuredly as you do so that with God a promise is always a promise and cannot ever possibly be otherwise. These promises cover the entire length of the Christian life from its beginning to its end and again and again they are focussed on and revolve around the Lord Jesus Christ and the 'unsearchable riches' (Ephesians 3:8) that are to be found in him. And as the Lord brings his promises to pass (as here at Bethany) he reveals so much more of himself to us and increases our 'joy and peace in believing' (Romans 15:13). Consider what the sorrowing ones here were to learn of the Saviour's compassion (as he wept at their brother's grave), his power (as he commanded the grave to give up the dead man), and his love (as he blessed the three of them together again in his presence).

It was a delay of power

The glory of Jesus, the wisdom of Jesus and now the power of Jesus—all of these were on wonderful display through Jesus' delay. Think of it this way regarding the power of Jesus: which of these would glorify God more—the healing of a sick man or the raising of a dead man? Surely the latter, without question. In what was to follow in due course (as recorded in verses 38–44), the Lord Jesus was to be seen as the conqueror of the grave, the victor over death, the one who came so that 'he might destroy the one who has the power of death, that is, the devil, and deliver all those who through fear of death were subject to lifelong slavery' (Hebrews 2:14–15). Supreme in this work would be his own death followed by his own resurrection, but there is a clear foretaste of these things in the event now before us.

And this as a reason sometimes for divine delays continues to apply, for God does not change, and 'Jesus Christ is the same yesterday and today and for ever' (Hebrews 13:8). He does all things well. He makes no mistakes. His timings are always perfect, and that must include his works of power. The little family at Bethany were to learn of Jesus' power as never before, as matters unfolded; and fundamental to this is the fact of Jesus' delay for those two days.

It was a delay of love

This is a case of last but by no means least. Jesus' love for the family has been stated explicitly twice already. The sisters made it the basis of their plea on their brother's behalf when they sent the message to Jesus: 'Lord, he whom you *love* is ill.' Then, two verses later, we are told: 'Now Jesus *loved* Martha and her sister and Lazarus.' Things could not be clearer. Yet as time went on, as the waiting in the home at Bethany continued, and as Lazarus grew weaker and weaker, how must the two anxious women have felt?

Seek to put yourself in their shoes (an impossible task, maybe, but try). Imagine how the sick one grew paler and more deathly looking by the hour. Imagine the tears (sometimes stifled, sometimes uncontrolled) of the concerned ones. Yet, in a strange way which maybe the occupants of that home were aware of, at least in some small measure, the Lord Jesus Christ was with them, just as he promises to be with us always (as he himself declares in Matthew 28:20). He knew what was going on in their hearts, minds and bodies. He was listening to their conversations, hearing their prayers and watching their tears. He observed exactly the moment when Lazarus died. He knew both what he *was* doing and what he *would* do, as he always does. He knew that Psalm 30:5 would be their experience soon enough: 'Weeping may tarry for the night, but joy comes with the morning.' So, yes, 'when he heard that Lazarus was ill, he stayed two days longer in the place where he was'; and yes, by the time he performed his mighty miracle Lazarus had 'been dead four days'. Yet, despite all this and everything else, his delay was a delay of love, and the timing of his arrival would be absolutely perfect, as we shall see as our journey through this chapter continues.

3

Jesus' chief priority

John 11:7–10

Are you walking in the light or stumbling in the night? The answer you give will be a revealing indicator of the true state of your soul.

So far here in John 11 we have considered Jesus' *matchless love* and his *perfect timing*. The verses before us now in this third part bring us to Jesus' *chief priority*. What did the Lord Jesus Christ always put first? What was of the greatest importance to him?

A couple of days have passed since the messenger returned from Jesus to Mary and Martha back in their home in Bethany. Throughout that time, Jesus has stayed where he was and has made no move towards Bethany. But just as his perfect timing is seen in his staying still, so it is seen also in his rising up.

Observe the flow of these few verses. We have:

Jesus' statement to his disciples (verse 7), 'Let us go to Judea again', a statement very much directed to test their courage, their mettle.

The disciples' response to Jesus (verse 8), 'Rabbi, the Jews were just now seeking to stone you, and you are going there again?' They were astounded at Jesus' proposal, fearing it to be extremely rash, and so opposed it. On what basis? That previous attempts upon his life were still fresh in their memories and it would be dangerous to be out and about again in Judea so soon. It may be that they were concerned for their own safety as well as his.

Jesus' reply to the disciples (verses 9–10 and beyond), the purpose of which was both to *reassure* them and to *challenge* them. The *reassurance* was to remind them that there are 'twelve hours in the day', twelve hours of daylight in which to be at work. As if to say, 'Don't be afraid of the Jews and their stones, or my life being cut short before its time: I'm like someone walking in the full light of day—I have not yet completed the entire season eternally decreed for me here on the earth; my 'day' of work is not yet over.' The *challenge* was to declare to them that to shrink from the clear call of God on account of the fear of man is like walking and stumbling in the dark. As if to say, 'So let us not be filled with fears of what anyone can do to us.' Hebrews 13:6 comes to mind: 'So we can confidently say, "The Lord is my helper; I will not fear; what can man do to me?"'

We may all often be tempted to shrink back when the call of God to us in Jesus is to press on, to go forward, to reach toward the mark, setting our face like a flint. Jesus would remind his disciples, and he would remind us, that (as the frequently quoted saying goes), we are immortal until our work is done. Hence the call to walk 'in the day' and 'not stumble', since we see 'the light of this world'. The only alternative? To walk 'in the night' and to stumble, since 'the light is not in' such. Recall Jesus' own words linking himself and those who truly belong to him and follow him: 'I am the light of the world. Whoever follows me will not walk in darkness, but will have the light of life.' (John 8:12.)

So then, let us focus more closely upon this matter of *Jesus' chief priority*, expressed in the question at the beginning of this present section. It is a searching question: are you walking in the light or stumbling in the night? What is the difference? How may we know, in order to give a true answer to that question? It is the difference between three pairs of things.

Fellowship with God and ignorance of God

To what have we been called as Christian believers? To nothing less than this: to know God and to have fellowship (or relationship) with him. Jesus tells us so himself in John 17:3. 'And this is eternal life, that they know you, the only true God, and Jesus Christ whom you have sent.' That is what it means to be a Christian! Knowing God, and having fellowship with God. Hearing God speak to us through his word, the Bible. Having conversation with God in prayer. And this applies not only in our more formal times of gathered public worship, but in the whole of life and throughout all of every day.

Before we became Christians, we did not know God—not in a personal way, not in an intimate manner. In Jesus' language here, we walked and stumbled 'in the night'. And if you are reading this and are still not yourself a Christian, then this is what you are still doing, right now. In such a condition there is nothing real, nothing living, nothing personal, nothing dynamic, nothing glorious between you and God. You are his creation. He made you and sustains you and he blesses you in many gracious ways. Yet you do not actually know him for yourself. Once you do know God, once you do possess Christ, you are brought from the darkness of night to the light of the day. The apostle Peter expresses this beautifully when he writes, 'that you may proclaim the excellencies of him who called you out of darkness into his marvellous light' (1 Peter 2:9).

Yet you may ask, perhaps, where in all of this does Jesus' chief priority come in? To which the answer is that it is in the amazing unity and mystery of what we call the Trinity (that God is one and God is three, the Father, the Son and the Holy Spirit). What was always the Son's chief priority and delight (and that word *chief* is key)? The answer: fellowship with the Father. A classic verse, Proverbs 8:30, declares this, where Jesus himself is speaking: '... and I was daily his delight, rejoicing before him always'. And the plain evidence of the gospels is that what was so there, in eternity, continued to be Jesus' chief priority and delight throughout the entire course of his earthly ministry. We discover that his fellowship with the Father (often rising up before the dawning of the day for prayer) is living in the light of his Father's presence (under the smile of his Father's favour and in the blessedness of his Father's company). And behind all of this, and richly illustrative of it, Jesus was always and remains always concerned (his chief priority and delight) that we should ourselves be taken up with the glory of God, in the absolute wonder of being in fellowship with him, and no longer remaining in ignorance of him. In our being born again, '... God, who said, "Let light shine out of darkness", has shone in our hearts to give the light of the knowledge of the glory of God in the face of Jesus Christ' (2 Corinthians 4:6). He would have *his* chief priority and delight be *our* chief priority and delight. Listen to his words in prayer to the Father. First, he prays, 'I glorified you on earth, having accomplished the work that you gave me to do. And now, Father, glorify me in your own presence with the glory that I had with you before the world existed.' (John 17:4–5.) Then, a little later in the same prayer, he prays, 'Father, I desire that they also, whom you have given me, may be with me where I am, to see my glory that you have given me because you loved me before the foundation of the world' (John 17:24).

In a word, we are to 'walk in the light, as he is in the light' (1 John 1:7). Do we?

Living for God and living for ourselves

Who do you live for? Who do you serve? Who are you most concerned to glorify? Whose will is it your main business to seek both to know and to do? In a word, does your life revolve around yourself (stumbling in the night) or around the Lord (walking in the light)?

What was the attitude of the Lord Jesus Christ for himself in such matters? This is what he tells us:

> 'Then I said, "Behold, I have come to do your will, O God, as it is written of me in the scroll of the book"' (Hebrews 10:7, quoting from what Jesus himself first declared in Psalm 40:7–8). 'Jesus said to them, "My food is to do the will of him who sent me and to accomplish his work"' (John 4:34). '"Father, if you are willing, remove this cup from me. Nevertheless, not my will, but yours, be done"' (Luke 22:42). 'I glorified you on earth, having accomplished the work that you gave me to do' (John 17:4).

His chief priority was at all times to serve and to glorify the Father, to know and to do the will of the Father, and to please the Father in everything.

How urgent, practical and constant true Christlikeness is! How he urges the very same priority upon those of us who are his disciples! Again, this is what he tells us:

> 'Do not labour for the food that perishes, but for the food that endures to eternal life, which the Son of Man will give to you. For on him God the Father has set his seal.' (John 6:27.) 'But seek first the kingdom of God and his righteousness, and all these things will be added to you' (Matthew 6:33). 'And you shall love the Lord your God with all your heart and with all your soul and with all your mind and with all your strength' (Mark 12:30).

Here's the heart of the matter: is your desire for the things that abide for ever (spiritual securities) or for the things that must fade and fail (worldly insecurities)? Are you still your own, or have you been 'bought with a price' (1 Corinthians 6:20), so that now you 'belong to another' (Romans 7:4)? Who do you live for, long for, and desire to please and glorify?

Spending eternity with God or spending eternity without him

We are told in Hebrews 12:2 that 'for the joy that was set before him' the Lord Jesus Christ 'endured the cross, despising the shame, and is seated at the right hand of the throne of God'. Pause for a moment to ask this question: what *was* this 'joy that was set before him'? Have you ever considered that? No doubt it comprised many things, some of which it is not ours to enter into—it would bear on the mystery and intimacy of the eternal relationship between the Father and the Son within the Godhead. Yet it must surely have included at least this: the joy he would know, experience and relish most fully in heaven of God being glorified in the gathering in of the whole church of God—all those for whom Jesus shed his blood and died, that 'great multitude that no one could number' (Revelation 7:9); the 'full-filling' of the great plan of redemption, established from 'before the foundation of the world' (Ephesians 1:4); the high day of rejoicing over all those sinners who have repented and returned to the Father's house, all the lost sheep who have been found, all the sons who were dead and are alive again.

It adds up to this: the joy of heaven, the joy of the glory of God in heaven, all of which was purchased at the awful cost of the sufferings, humiliation and death of the Lord Jesus Christ himself on the cross of Calvary (he who 'himself bore our sins in his body on the tree, that we might die to sin and live to righteousness', 1 Peter 2:24; he who 'also suffered once for sins, the righteous for the unrighteous, that he might bring us to God', 1 Peter 3:18). And how was this ever possible? Only through the free grace of God to sinners. 'For by grace you have been saved through faith. And this is not your own doing; it is the gift of God, not a result of works, so that no one may boast' (Ephesians 2:8–9).

How the Son of God looked forward to that. It signified the completing of his work, his returning to the Father, his crowning day in heaven. And this very verse, Hebrews 12:2, urges us to be 'looking to Jesus', to be fixing our eyes upon him, to 'consider him' (Hebrews 12:3). To what purpose? That *his* priority and delight would be *our* priority and delight, not earthbound but heavenbound, not 'stumbling in the night' without him but 'walking in the light' in company with him, all the way to heaven.

The stark alternatives are set forth with remarkable clarity and force in Proverbs 4:18–19: 'But the path of the righteous is like the light of dawn, which shines brighter and brighter until full day. The way of the wicked is like deep darkness; they do not know over what they stumble'. So flee from the darkness (if that is where you are) and come to the light (which is where you need to be). Be finished with 'stumbling in the night'. Now is the time—it is always the time—to be 'walking in the light'.

4

Jesus' comprehensive knowledge

John 11:11

Jesus, as we have been considering, is talking to his disciples. Time is passing since the news reached him of his friend Lazarus' illness. Still he has not set off to Bethany. There emerges now, however, a hint of impending movement. 'After saying these things, he said to them, "Our friend Lazarus has fallen asleep, but I go to awaken him"' (verse 11). By 'fallen asleep' Jesus meant that Lazarus had died. The disciples did not grasp this immediately (as the next verses make plain). They got completely the wrong end of the stick. Focusing for now, however, upon the present verse at the head of this section, the wonderfully striking and gloriously profound fact is that when Jesus declared that 'Lazarus has fallen asleep', he knew that he had died. No one had informed him. The message from the sisters did not say this, for when they wrote it their brother was still alive. He just knew. And how did he know? Because the man, the real man Christ Jesus is the Son of God, the Lord of glory, the one who knows all things, even 'the secrets of the heart' (Psalm 44:21).

We may speak of this as *Jesus' comprehensive knowledge*, or what is called his *omniscience*. This is one of the clearest evidences in the Gospels of Jesus' deity, or divinity. Jesus' knowledge is not partial or bitty, but complete, full-orbed, total and all-embracing. Scripture treats this on a grand scale, assuring us that in him 'are hidden all the treasures of wisdom and knowledge' (Colossians 2:3). He says of himself, 'I am the Alpha and the Omega, the first and the last, the beginning and the end' (Revelation 22:13). He knows 'what was in man' (John 2:25).

In this part of our study, however, we shall not deal with the grand scale treatment but focus rather upon this knowledge in its more personal applications, because this verse 11 is highly personal. It concerns his knowledge of his own, remembering that, 'The Lord knows those who are his' (2 Timothy 2:19), and (his own assertion as the good shepherd of his sheep), 'I know my own and my own know me' (John 10:14).

So what does Jesus know about us? In one word, everything. But consider these four things in particular: He knows our name, he knows our sins, he knows our frame, and he knows our dying.

He knows our name

Child of God, the Lord Jesus Christ knows exactly who you are. Could anything be more amazing and comforting than that? 'Our friend *Lazarus*'—not some unnamed character or anonymous person, but Lazarus. The disciples, for all that they are puzzled at what Jesus will say, are not left asking him who he means. 'Our friend' is heart-warming on its own, but when his personal name, Lazarus, follows, this takes it to another level altogether.

The Lord has many friends. In the upper room, he said to his disciples, 'I have called you friends' (John 15:15). He knows each one of us by name, and never confuses us with one another. He never forgets who we are; he is not like those people who tell us that they are no good with names. Jesus is perfect with names, just as he is perfect with everything else. Our name is never just on the tip of his tongue but getting no further. He has no difficulty placing us. He knows our name, he knows our person.

This is worth unpacking a little more.

He knew us by name when God (the Father) 'chose us in him [the Son] before the foundation of the world' (Ephesians 1:4).

He knew us by name when, in the eternal counsel of the Godhead, he agreed to leave heaven's glory for a season, making himself nothing, and coming to earth for us (Philippians 2:6–8).

He knew us by name when he suffered and died on the cross, where 'he loved me and gave himself for me' (Galatians 2:20).

And because he knows us by name, he will never lose us or mislay us. He assures us of this. 'And this is the will of him who sent me, that I should lose nothing of all that he has given me, but raise it up on the last day' (John 6:39).

He knows our sins

He speaks of 'Our *friend* Lazarus'. The one who speaks is the 'friend of … sinners' (Matthew 11:19), a name thrown at him there in abuse, but little did the abusers realise what they were saying!

Jesus knows our sins. Maybe that strikes you as an alarming thought, fearing that you can hardly be his friend if he knows the whole truth about you, inside and out. You could look at it that way, but here is a much better (and a much more Christ-glorifying way) to look at it. Instead of being alarmed, be thankful: thankful that the Lord Jesus, knowing your sins (and everything else about you, even the smallest or apparently hidden detail), still calls you his friend! Well may we be thoroughly ashamed of our sins and rightly so. But consider these two things:

Firstly, when Jesus chose us, when he loved us, he knew everything about us. He observed our utter ruin on account of the Fall. People speak of love sometimes as being 'blind' but that can never be said about Jesus' love. Both of his eyes are wide open and clear-sighted, and yet he loves us.

Secondly, having saved us he knows us still. He knows the coldness of our hearts towards him so much of the time, the poverty of our service for him, the inadequacy of our worship of him, and the glaring lack of our likeness to him (even after, for some of us, many, many years of being a Christian). He loves us with a love that will not let us go. He loves us with a love which is for ever and ever. And still he calls us his friends.

He knows our frame

It is impossible to make that statement without recalling Psalm 103:14: 'For he knows our frame; he remembers that we are dust.' This is a most blessed thing—'our frame', how we are formed—which gathers up a number of thoughts.

He knows all our trials. Maybe there is a particular trial under which you are bowed at the moment, a particular extremity that you are facing as a child of God, a particular perplexity that it seems utterly beyond you to resolve, a particular hill of difficulty that you are having to climb, a particular cup of suffering that you are being baptised with. The triune God knows all your trials. The Lord Jesus Christ suffered multiple trials. This was a wonderful comfort to Job in his many heavy trials. This is what he tells us: 'But he knows the way that I take; when he has tried me, I shall come out as gold' (Job 23:10).

He knows all our pains. They come in so many varied shapes and sizes; bodily, physical, mental, emotional; disappointment, heartbreak, fear, friends turning against you and speaking ill of you, people misunderstanding what you are seeking to do; the list goes on. The triune God knows all your pains. The Lord Jesus Christ suffered multiple pains.

He knows exactly what we can bear, how much we can carry. 1 Corinthians 10:13 assures us of this. 'No temptation has overtaken you that is not common to man. God is faithful, and he will not let you be tempted beyond your ability, but with the temptation he will also provide the way of escape, that you may be able to endure it.' Think of Lazarus here in our present context. His strength was fading, colour will have been draining from his face, his very life itself appeared to be ebbing away. Think of Mary and Martha, with their grief over their brother's condition and (no doubt) their perplexity over there still being no sign of Jesus' arrival in response to their urgent message (even though he had sent word to them that Lazarus' 'illness does not lead to death'). It is a sad scene. Yet the Lord knew all about it, and had not in any way forgotten them, neither was he in any way neglecting them. He knows our constitution, because he made us. We are 'fearfully and wonderfully made' (Psalm 139:14). He knows whether we are by nature weak or strong, bold or timid, anxious or without a care, weary or vigorous. The triune God knows all your circumstances. The Lord Jesus Christ suffered real human experiences, trials and temptations, 'who in every respect has been tempted as we are, yet without sin' (Hebrews 4:15).

He knows when Satan is pressing us hard. He is wholly aware of all the fears and dangers that the evil one seeks to cause us and does cause us. The triune God knows all your circumstances and vulnerabilities arising from these attacks. The Lord Jesus Christ suffered constant personal assaults from Satan. And with regard to those that came his way right at the start of Jesus' public ministry, the devil (realising that on that occasion he could not defeat the Son of God) only 'departed from him until an opportune time' (Luke 4:13).

He knows our dying

What did Jesus say to his disciples? 'Our friend Lazarus has fallen asleep ….' The disciples did not grasp this, but Jesus knew precisely what was happening and what he intended to do, 'that the Son of God may be glorified through it' (verse 4). True, the Lord Jesus was not there physically in the little home in Bethany. But Jesus' *friend* Lazarus had died, and Jesus knew it. Lazarus' death, of course, was subsequent to his sisters' message, at which point he was clearly seriously ill but still alive. Now he was dead. Jesus knew that.

He knows our being born and our dying, for both have been appointed by God from eternity. Yet there is a special (and beautiful) reason why he knows our dying. Psalm 116:15 tells us what that is: 'Precious in the sight of the LORD is the death of his saints.' It is a most precious thing to the good shepherd when one of his sheep dies. Precious? How so? For reasons like these.

Precious because we have belonged to him for ever. Ephesians 1:3–4 reminds us that we have been blessed 'in Christ with every spiritual blessing in the heavenly places, even as he [God the Father] chose us in him [God the Son] before the foundation of the world, that we should be holy and blameless before him'.

Precious because he has bought us for himself at an unimaginably great price. That price? His own blood. 'You are not your own, for you were bought with a price' (1 Corinthians 6:19–20). We have been redeemed 'with the precious blood of Christ, like that of a lamb without blemish or spot' (1 Peter 1:19). Note that: precious blood for those precious to Jesus!

Precious because of Jesus' own desire for us. This truth is expressed most exquisitely in Jesus' own words in prayer to his Father, recorded for our blessing and assurance in John 17:24: 'Father, I desire that they also, whom you have given me, may be with me where I am, to see my glory that you have given me because you loved me before the foundation of the world.'

These are some of the glorious things behind that verse from Psalm 116. They applied to Lazarus. They apply to all those who believe and trust in the Lord Jesus Christ. They apply to you, dear reader, if that is true of you. Moreover, a remarkable verse (Ecclesiastes 7:1) assures every true believer that 'the day of death is better than the day of birth'. The death of a believer is not some tragic event, not even (to be said sensitively) an untimely event. It is a precious event, a precious death, an excellent and honourable event. Jesus knows our dying, and undertakes to assist and accompany us in it and through it.

Let us take this to heart. 'For none of us lives to himself, and none of us dies to himself. For if we live, we live to the Lord, and if we die, we die to the Lord. So then, whether we live or whether we die, we are the Lord's. For to this end Christ died and lived again, that he might be Lord both of the dead and of the living.' (Romans 14:7–9.)

This is an aspect of what we have called *Jesus' comprehensive knowledge*. What should (must) be our only correct response? To praise and adore him. To cast all our care upon him. To seek never to offend him. And to keep constantly before our hearts the day when we shall see him and be made like him, asking the Holy Spirit to create in us a sincere and fervent longing for that day! And if you should be reading these lines and (as yet) know nothing of these things, think seriously and deeply upon them now, and may the Lord be pleased to open your eyes, draw near to you, save you, and make these amazing realities your very own!

5

Jesus' remarkable picture

John 11:11–16

As the narrative unfolds, a demanding question awaits all who read it. How do you think of death? Or maybe a prior question needs to be asked: *Do you think of death*? Without doubt, death has a great seriousness and awesomeness about it, and it is not enough to brush it off with a vague 'everyone has to come to it eventually'. Scripture refers to it as 'the king of terrors' (Job 18:14) and 'The last enemy' (1 Corinthians 15:26). Yet here in John 11, Jesus uses a very different picture to speak of death. He likens it to falling asleep, saying, 'Our friend Lazarus has fallen asleep …'. What a contrast with the descriptions in the two Bible verses just quoted.

To 'sleep' was the common expression for the death of the saints in the Old Testament. God told Moses that he would sleep (or 'lie down') with his fathers (Deuteronomy 31:16). Job declared that he would sleep 'in the earth' (Job 7:21). Daniel 12:2 affirms that 'many of those who sleep in the dust of the earth shall awake, some to everlasting life, and some to shame and everlasting contempt'.

Why the difference between the first pair of verses quoted, and the second trio? What can account for this radical change in language? The reason is very plain. Death, considered in itself, is a terrible thing. In that first text, Job speaks of being 'torn from the tent in which he trusted' (18:14). It represents a rending, a tearing apart, a leaving behind. Death, of course, exists solely as a result of sin. If there had been no sin there would be no death. Paul makes this absolutely clear when he writes, 'Therefore, just as sin came into the world through one man, and death through sin, and so death spread to all men because all sinned …' (Romans 5:12). He is taking us right back to Adam and Eve in the Garden of Eden. Death, with sin, speaks of curse, misery, bondage, punishment, separation from God, terrors, judgment, the unknown, and deep heart-rending sorrow. And we must all face it. It is the one thing of which we may all be sure. For 'it is appointed for man to die once, and after that comes judgment' (Hebrews 9:27).

In the light of all this, then, how can Jesus speak of dying as falling asleep? It is a warm, comforting, encouraging, hopeful, welcome description. The answer is that he is using this phrase exclusively of those who love him and belong to him, those whose Saviour from sin he is, those whom he has delivered from judgment, those whose sins have been forgiven on account of his death upon the cross, those to whom he has given the free gift of eternal life through his resurrection from the dead. In a word, they are sinners who have been reconciled to God through him. They are 'the ransomed of the LORD' (Isaiah 35:10). They are those of whom 'a voice from heaven' speaks: 'Blessed are the dead who die in the Lord …' (Revelation 14:13).

The key focus of this present section (verses 11–16) is this matter of death as falling asleep. Link together these two statements of Jesus: 'Our friend Lazarus *has fallen asleep*' (emphasis mine) and 'Lazarus *has died*' (emphasis mine). Lazarus is the one loved by Jesus (stated back in verse 3), and who is Jesus' friend. And this confronts us with what is a regular and consistent biblical distinction, the difference between those who are the people of God and those who are not, those who are the friends of Christ and those who are not, those whose sins have been forgiven and those whose sins have not. All the time there is this gulf, and we are all on one side of it or the other. There is no middle position or halfway house.

This picture of death as falling asleep, therefore, is true *only* of the Christian, the one who has fallen asleep in Jesus. That is to say, trusting in him, leaning on him, confident in him, resting in him, believing in him, hoping in him (his person, his work, his merits, his blood, his righteousness); Jesus only and Jesus completely. Dear reader, if you are not in this happy position, then death must remain for you the 'king of terrors' to which you must one day be marched away.

Let us seek to open up *Jesus' remarkable picture* somewhat and explore it further. It speaks to us of at least four things:

The harmlessness of death for the Christian

You have to die if you are a Christian, just as everyone else has to die. That is a given. Being a Christian does not somehow exempt you from death, or enable you to skip it or avoid it. The only exception to that is for those who are still alive on earth at the return of the Lord Jesus. Their experience is clarified in 1 Thessalonians 4:17, and is reminiscent of Enoch and Elijah.

The point, however, is this (and it is a grand one!): dying and death cannot harm you. Jesus uses the image of sleep, something we can all readily identify with. Like sleep, death for the Christian is a friend and not a foe. But what of its sting, something which Paul refers to in 1 Corinthians 15:56: 'The sting of death'? What of its power? What of its threats? What of its terrors? To all these questions the magnificent and triumphant answer is that Jesus has dealt with them all. How so? In his death upon the cross. We quoted from the verse that says 'The sting of death is sin …', and at the cross Jesus dealt with our sin and our sins. In his resurrection from the dead, by which he vanquished death, he destroyed 'the one who has the power of death, that is, the devil' (Hebrews 2:14). So through his death and resurrection Jesus has done all that is needed to 'deliver all those who through fear of death were subject to lifelong slavery' (Hebrews 2:15).

Back to 1 Corinthians 15, this time verses 54–55 & 57:

> '"… Death is swallowed up in victory.
> O death, where is your victory?
> O death, where is your sting?" …
>
> But thanks be to God, who gives us the victory through our Lord Jesus Christ.'

The fearlessness of death for the Christian

Returning to the image of sleep, recall Jesus' words to his disciples, 'Our friend Lazarus has fallen asleep, but I go to awaken him.' Are you afraid of sleep? No? Is it not particularly welcome when it provides you (at least for a few hours) with relief from pains and sorrows? Then why, if you are a Christian, are you afraid of death, if only from the consideration that it will provide you with eternal relief from all the pains and sorrows of your present life—for it will take you immediately to be with Christ in heaven, where pains and sorrows are no more? We have no need to be afraid. A verse just quoted assures of this, for Jesus is the one (the only one, but there is no need for any other) who can deliver us from the 'fear of death', so that we are no longer left in bondage and slavery to it.

Yet we need to be honest with ourselves and with one another, for we *are* sometimes fearful, or at least apprehensive. Is that not so? Maybe it is because we do not get the opportunity for a 'practice run' at it, or because we have witnessed Christian family or friends having a struggling death (either because of great physical pain and weakness, or because of attacks of Satan upon their assurance). Or maybe, speaking frankly, it is because we are not believing the promises of the gospel as we ought to, or not resting sufficiently upon the finished work of Jesus on our behalf. In which case, our earnest cry must be, 'I believe; help my unbelief!' (Mark 9:24).

If we are fearful, then we need to acknowledge our fears openly before the Lord. There is no shame in doing this. There is no use in pretending we do not have fear—that is mere pride. Doing so will, hopefully, both challenge and encourage us, showing us the unreasonableness of such fears and enabling us to realise that to continue with them both dishonours our Saviour and hinders ourselves. What rich blessing it would be to learn, once and for all, that if we truly are children of God, then our fears over death are just not necessary. A fresh dose of Isaiah 12:1–3 should always do us great good— a passage, dear reader, which you can look up and relish for yourself!

Before going on, one more comment that is perhaps the most important of all. Mention was made a couple of paragraphs ago of the fact that, in the very way of things, we only go this way once—we have not travelled the way of dying and death before. That is absolutely true, but *always remember* that there *is* one who *has* been this way before. And he has done so not only himself but specifically for us. The Lord Jesus Christ! So, when we die, we go the way he has already gone. This is a wonderful aspect of *our union with Christ in his death and then in his resurrection.*

The restfulness of death for the Christian

Sleep speaks, among other things, of rest, relief and refreshment. It provides *rest* for our bodies; *relief* from the toils, labours and sorrows of the day; and *refreshment* for our whole being, including minds and spirits, with a view to further duties when we awake.

Surely this applies very naturally to the sleep of death. Revelation 14:13 is a precious verse for every believer, to believe now and experience hereafter: 'And I heard a voice from heaven saying, "Write this: Blessed are the dead who die in the Lord from now on." "Blessed indeed," says the Spirit, "that they may rest from their labours …."'

The change from life on earth to life in heaven is massive and radical. Throughout our Christian lives (whether short or long) we need constantly to 'be strong in the Lord and in the strength of his might', moment by moment putting 'on the whole armour of God, that [we] may be able to stand against the schemes of the devil' (Ephesians 6:10–11). Here, we must obey the Christian's 'standing orders': '… pray without ceasing …. Do not quench the Spirit. … test everything. … Abstain from every form of evil.' (1 Thessalonians 5:17, 19, 21–22.) Here, it is our priority to 'put on the Lord Jesus Christ, and make no provision for the flesh, to gratify its desires' (Romans 13:14).

When, through grace, we come at last to heaven, things will be altogether different. None of the activities just mentioned will occupy us any longer. Faith will have vanished into sight. Heavenly joys will replace earthly sorrows. Pure worship will take the place of our fall-short offerings here. In a word, we shall at last discover what we were told all along: our present 'light momentary affliction' really will have given way to 'an eternal weight of glory beyond all comparison' (2 Corinthians 4:17). We shall have been brought safely to the fulfilment of the lovely promise of Hebrews 4:9, that 'there remains a Sabbath rest for the people of God'.

The hopefulness of death for the Christian

Hopefulness? Yes, indeed! Think of 'Christ in you, the hope of glory' (Colossians 1:27). What is your hope, anticipation and expectation after having fallen asleep and being refreshed, as night is followed by the morning of a new day? Surely, that you will wake up! Well, there is a most glorious vein of spiritual application from Jesus' description here in John 11 of a believer's death as falling asleep. You fall asleep and you wake up!

Observe verse 11 again, where Jesus says of Lazarus, 'I go to awaken him' (a clear reference to the fact that he had died, for Jesus would not be merely waking him up from ordinary sleep after the time that had now elapsed). Notwithstanding the particular circumstances at Bethany, this is a picture of the sure fact that for every believer we not only 'fall asleep' when we die, but that falling asleep is followed by a waking up. This waking up has two stages: immediately, upon death, into the presence of the Saviour ('away from the body and at home with the Lord', 2 Corinthians 5:8), then at the general resurrection at the last day, upon Christ's return ('for an hour is coming when all who are in the tombs will hear his voice and come out' John 5:28–29). The first stage involves the separation of soul and body for a season. The second stage sees the reunion of soul and body, but a resurrection body ('... sown a natural body; it is raised a spiritual body', 1 Corinthians 15:44).

The believer's 'sleep' is not an unconscious thing. By no means! If it *were* so, then how could Paul's desire be 'to depart and be with Christ, for that is far better' (Philippians 1:23)? Or how could David testify, 'As for me, I shall behold your face in righteousness; when I awake, I shall be satisfied with your likeness' (Psalm 17:15)? Or how could Isaiah speak of 'Your eyes will behold the king in his beauty; they will see a land that stretches afar [of far horizons]' (Isaiah 33:17)?

Sadly, the disciples did not really follow what Jesus was saying to them, hence the ensuing conversation in verses 12–16—'they thought that he meant taking rest in sleep'. But, as ever, the Lord Jesus bore patiently with them (just as he does with us), and explained things. 'Lazarus has died, and for your sake I am glad that I was not there, so that you may believe. But let us go to him.' In all that he does with us in our lives, Jesus intends that it should be for the growth to fuller maturity of our belief and trust in him.

And so the scene is set for Jesus to go to Bethany. Just before we head off there, however, do remember clearly that the harmlessness, the fearlessness, the restfulness and the hopefulness of death only applies to those who are Christians, those who are among Jesus' friends. Is that you?

6

Jesus' mighty help

John 11:17–22

One of the particular beauties of Scripture (and a keen testimony to its divine inspiration) is the way in which, so many times, one portion sheds light on another. They link together and illuminate one another. We have a delightful instance of this as we proceed now a little further into this marvellous chapter, John 11, and consider *Jesus' mighty help*.

This might immediately take our thought to Psalm 89:19, where God declares, 'I have granted help to one who is mighty.' That may also be translated either, 'I have laid help on a mighty one', or, 'I have given the capacity to be a help to a mighty one', with 'mighty' being the same word used in 'Mighty God' in Isaiah 9:6 (where it speaks of the Lord Jesus Christ). With respect to this psalm, while in the context there God is speaking in the first instance of David, yet we are correct to be drawn on to the Lord Jesus, of whom in many (not all) respects David is a 'type'. In the light of this, then, we do not hesitate to say that the deeper and ultimate reference of Psalm 89:19 is to the Son of God, the second person of the Trinity, our Lord and Saviour Jesus Christ. For us (wonder of wonders!), the Father has provided Jesus to be our true help, and he is a 'mighty' help. It is in this precious light that we get a further sight of the Saviour in John 11:17–22.

There are here what we might call two movements: Jesus going to Bethany to help and Martha going to Jesus for help. Let us explore each a little in turn.

Jesus went to Bethany to help

It will be remembered that when Jesus had received the poignant message from Mary and Martha, 'Lord, he whom you love is ill', he had not moved from where he was at the time. He did not rush to Bethany as fast as he could. He waited and he did so deliberately, knowing precisely what he *was doing* and what he *would do*.

Verse 17 opens with his arrival. Now he has come, arriving at Bethany (some two miles or so from Jerusalem) four days after Lazarus had died and been buried. It is important to note that the statement that Jesus 'found that Lazarus had already been in the tomb four days' does not mean (*most certainly* does not mean) that he discovered to his surprise that this was so, for he had already told his disciples that Lazarus was dead. Rather it declares as a matter of fact that it was so. In other words, it is there for our benefit, not his!

Why has Jesus come? Essentially because Mary and Martha were there. We were told back in verse 5 that 'Jesus loved Martha and her sister and Lazarus'. He came now on a visit of love. He came, as Hebrews 4:16 so exquisitely expresses it, that the grieving sisters would 'receive mercy and find grace to help in time of need'. And what a 'time of need' it certainly was for them, for that family of three siblings was as close and tight-knit as we could imagine.

He came with timely help, for such his help always is. He came to perform a mighty miracle in the raising of their brother from his grave. He came thereby to display a glorious sign (for all who had eyes to see) that he, the Lord Jesus, is the Lord of life and the Lord over death. To show that, in his own words of himself, 'I have the keys of Death …' (Revelation 1:18). He came 'to console them concerning their brother' (verse 19)—to console them with the power, grace and reality of the living God. He came to proclaim by word and deed the very gospel of God—timely help to perishing sinners around him who were in desperate need of salvation. In this connection we are supplied with the detail that 'many of the Jews' had come to the sisters' home.

Much later in the chapter we will learn of some very varying responses to this 'gospel' aspect of his visit. Verses 45 and following spell this out. But the great thing for now is that Jesus was there; there to bring heavenly comfort to the sorrowing sisters; there to bring gospel hope to others who had gathered. What a gracious visit it was in every way!

We observed that there are two movements in this section. Before passing to the second, however, consider again what the Father says of the Son in Psalm 89:19, and the connection between 'help' and 'mighty'. And who is this 'one' upon whom the Father has laid help for his people? He is 'the Son of God' (John 11:4). He is 'the Lord of glory' (1 Corinthians 2:8). He is 'King of kings and Lord of lords' (Revelation 19:16). Comprehensively stated, he is 'Wonderful Counsellor, Mighty God, Everlasting Father, Prince of Peace' (Isaiah 9:6).

What a help, our ever-timely help! Dear reader, do you know him as *your* help? Do you possess in him, this mighty help, the Saviour from sin, the giver of life, the victor over Satan and the conqueror of death? Do his comforts both fill and thrill your soul, especially in your darkest days? Has he made you glad? Pause and consider. And, dear child of God, have you not found the Lord Jesus to be all of this for you and to you, and much else besides?

Martha went to Jesus for help

How these two dear sisters must have been watching, wondering and waiting; weeping and grieving; wishing and hoping. They had received the very hopeful message just a few days before, yet it must have presented them with a puzzle as time passed. After all, Jesus had told them quite specifically that Lazarus' 'illness does not lead to death', and now he has died and been buried, and there has been no sign of Jesus. Were they confused?

But now things are starting to happen. Is light about to dawn for them, for 'Martha heard that Jesus was coming' (verse 20)? And what was her response? Straightaway, without any hesitation, fuss or noise, she slipped out of the house and set off down the road. We are told that 'she went and met him, but Mary remained seated in the house'. Indeed she actually left the village in the direction of his arrival, for verse 30 informs us that 'Jesus had not yet come into the village' at the point 'where Martha had met him'.

We are informed from verse 21 that when she and Jesus met, Martha was the first to speak. There appear to be three strands to what she said, strands which we may call reverence, devotion and confusion.

Martha shows her reverence for Jesus

She calls him 'Lord', which is far more than 'Sir' or a mere term of respect. 'Reverence' is the word which best captures it. In this she does us a favour, for her manner of address to Jesus reminds us that *all* our comings before the Lord (however heavy our spirits, confused our understandings, great our extremities or wretched our sins) must be *reverent* comings and approaches. We seek his presence and his mighty help not in order to parade ourselves before him but to bow down low, humble ourselves, even fall on our face before him. Let us learn and learn well from Martha. Coming in all the anguish, perplexity and longing of her heart, she (as it were) casts herself at Jesus' feet, always the very best place for us to be.

Martha shows her devotion to Jesus

It is important not to misunderstand what Martha says to Jesus here. In her words, 'if you had been here, my brother would not have died', she is not meaning something along the lines of 'Where have you been? What's your game? What are you playing at? This is a fine how-do-you-do, isn't it?' In no way is she implying that she thinks Jesus has some explaining to do. Forget completely any such motives in her speech. Martha is not complaining to Jesus; she is not taking him to task. Rather, she was expressing face to face before him what must often have been upon her and her sister's hearts over the past few days: 'If only Jesus was here!'

There were the other comforters and consolers (mentioned in verse 19), but they could only offer so much. They were no doubt well intentioned and of a different breed altogether from Job's famous 'comforters'. Only the Lord, however, can truly 'bind up the brokenhearted' (Isaiah 61:1), and raise 'up all who are bowed down' (Psalm 145:14). The sisters must surely (and understandably) have been thinking, and saying to each other, 'Oh that Jesus would come!', and we can understand this. Well has it been observed that 'afflicting time is trying time'. We have no wish to chide the women. In similar circumstances we seek to rally round and do all that we can. But *we are limited*, whereas *Jesus is limitless*. And how thankful we are that he is!

Martha shows her confusion to Jesus

That is meant in a kindly way. The thing is, it just was not the case that Lazarus would not have died if Jesus had been there; not automatically the case, anyway. Martha made the mistake of limiting Jesus 'by distance', as if everything depended upon his literal 'being there' in Bethany. It is interesting to remember the various occasions in the Gospels when Jesus performed miracles at a distance—the centurion's servant in Luke 7 and the official's son in John 4 are beautiful examples. A verse in Jeremiah's prophecy (23:23) is also pertinent: "Am I a God at hand, declares the LORD, and not a God far away?"

What dear Martha lacked at this point was a God-glorifying, faith-strengthening, hope-enlivening grasp of the glorious relationship between the Father and the Son. For although she was able to go on to utter her conviction recorded in verse 22, ('But even now I know that whatever you ask from God, God will give you'), which looks promising, evidently the word she used there for 'ask' is a particular word which implies an *inferior* making a request of a *superior*. It is a verb which Jesus never used himself in his requests before his Father. The word *he* used was one implying the equality of the one who asks with the one who is asked. That is thoroughly appropriate because the Lord Jesus Christ is God and the Father can never deny or turn away his Son!

Let it be said on the positive side, however, that Martha did show a faith and a confidence in Jesus with her 'even now'. Amid her gloom (Lazarus being dead and gone), there is a ray of hope still that the mysterious message of verse 4 about Lazarus' sickness not ending in death and all turning out to the glory of God, will yet have a happy and a blessed result. She shows the classic mix in Christian experience of grace and weakness, faith and unbelief, just like the rest of us who name the name of Jesus. And there's this, too: maybe she knew Psalm 89:19, and was hanging on tightly to it!

May we all be enabled to do the same. If you are not yet a Christian, seek the Lord Jesus as your one and true mighty help, to convict you of your sin and uncleanness before God, to give you 'a broken and contrite heart' (Psalm 51:17), to save you from all your sin and provide for you peace with God. While, if you are already a Christian, go on day by day, moment by moment, circumstance by circumstance, seeking the Lord Jesus as your one and true mighty help, to enable you to walk in a holy and blameless way before the Lord, to 'guide you continually' (Isaiah 58:11), to give you a firmer grasp upon his promises and grant you blessed assurance of salvation.

Either way, go to Jesus, and keep on going to Jesus, for in him and with him is all the *mighty help* you can ever possibly need!

7

Jesus' powerful intercession

John 11:22

Three questions: Where is Jesus now? How did he get there? What is he doing there? These three questions, between them, take us to the heart of something of immense significance as we linger a little longer with what Martha says to Jesus in verse 22: 'But even now I know that whatever you ask from God, God will give you'. In these words, Martha puts her finger right on the spot.

Where is Jesus now? He is in heaven, seated 'at the right hand of the Majesty on high' (Hebrews 1:3).

How did he get there? Through his death, resurrection and ascension. 'The God of our fathers raised Jesus, whom you killed by hanging him on a tree. God exalted him at his right hand…' (Acts 5:30–31).

What is he doing there? The answer needs to be a multiple one. He is governing the universe; 'he upholds the universe by the word of his power' (Hebrews 1:3). He is building and preserving his church: '… I will build my church, and the gates of hell shall not prevail against it' (Matthew 16:18). He is preparing heaven for the arrival of his people; 'In my Father's house are many rooms. If it were not so, would I have told you that I go to prepare a place for you?' (John 14:2.) And he is doing so much more, such as welcoming 'those who have fallen asleep [that is, died trusting in him]' (1 Thessalonians 4:14); giving gifts to his church and equipping us for service: 'When he ascended on high he led a host of captives, and he gave gifts to men' (Ephesians 4:8, quoting Psalm 68:18). He dwells in his church as her head: '… I saw seven golden lampstands, and in the midst of the lampstands one like a son of man …' (Revelation 1:12–13). He is preparing for his own glorious return at the end of the age: 'waiting for our blessed hope, the appearing of the glory of our great God and Saviour Jesus Christ' (Titus 2:13).

Something else remains, however, in our answer to this third question, and it is one of the most important things of all. He is engaging in earnest and continual prayer for his people. Among places where this is stated are Romans 8:34 ('… Christ Jesus is the one who died—more than that, who was raised—who is at the right hand of God, who indeed is interceding for us') and Hebrews 7:25 ('… since he always lives to make intercession for them').

We speak of this as the intercessory ministry of the Lord Jesus Christ. It is the ongoing part of his ministry as our 'great high priest' (Hebrews 4:14). Note that word, *ongoing* (or, *continuing*). There are two distinct aspects to Jesus' high priestly ministry, the finished part and the ongoing part. The *finished* part focuses on the cross, where Jesus uttered the matchless words, 'It is finished' (John 19:30—three words in English, one in Greek). He had done all, accomplished all, for the salvation of his people, all the 'types' and prophecies pertaining to the provision for us of 'such a great salvation' (Hebrews 2:3). Now that he is in heaven *as* our great and glorious high priest, Jesus is engaged in this continual prayerfulness, this unceasing intercession for his own. Just as the names of the tribes of Israel were engraved upon 'the two stones on the shoulder pieces of the ephod, as stones of remembrance for the sons of Israel', to the end that 'Aaron [the high priest] shall bear their names before the LORD' (Exodus 28:12), even so the Lord Jesus Christ, our incomparable high priest, ever bears our names upon his heart before the Father. Surely we are standing here upon the most wonderfully comforting, assuring and encouraging ground!

Arising, then, from this John 11 context of Martha's words to Jesus, let us explore something of *Jesus' powerful intercession*. And as we do so, it is important to say that, in this genuine expression of faith from Martha's lips, there was something lacking in what she said. Note her words carefully: '... whatever you *ask* from God, God will give you.' I have already highlighted that verb '*ask*'. The word she used is a word for prayer which is proper upon the lips of an *in*ferior making a request or asking a favour of a *su*perior. Jesus himself, when in prayer, never used that word. The word he used is one which ordinarily implies the equality of the two persons (the one asking and the one being asked). Obviously that is far more proper in the case of Jesus praying to the Father, since all three persons of the Godhead (Father, Son and Holy Spirit) are co-equal and co-eternal, equal in power and glory. Just think of what Jesus says in John 10:30, 'I and the Father are one'. Not least, they are altogether one in will and purpose.

The Son asking the Father

Martha says to Jesus, 'Whatever you ask from God.' What may we say of this? Let us observe four things:

Jesus asks at the Father's invitation

There is no imposition here on the Son's part, no speaking out of turn, no taking liberties. As far back as Psalm 2:8 the Father had said to the Son, 'Ask of me, and I will make the nations your heritage, and the ends of the earth your possession.' There is the greatest oneness and intimacy imaginable between the Father and the Son (a oneness and intimacy from which the Holy Spirit is in no way exempt, of course).

Jesus asks as our great high priest

We have just stated that there is this distinction in the Lord Jesus' priestly work between that which is finished and that which continues, that which is 'past-completed' and that which is 'present-active'. 'For Christ has entered, not into holy places made with hands, which are copies of the true things, but into heaven itself, now to appear in the presence of God on our behalf' (Hebrews 9:24).

Jesus asks for us, now that he is in heaven, those things which he asked for us on earth

I put it that way, because we might very reasonably ask the question, 'Fine, that's wonderful, the Lord Jesus Christ prays for us, but how can we ever have any idea of *what* he prays for us?' Thankfully, Jesus does not leave us in the dark on this matter.

The richest and deepest seam of his intercession for us while he was on earth must surely be the whole of John 17, which is often referred to as his high priestly prayer. Since 'Jesus Christ is the same yesterday and today and forever' (Hebrews 13:8), we may learn from his *earthly* praying some of the subjects of his *heavenly* praying. Pause and take a moment to read John 17 through now.

From that chapter, we may glean the following as some of Jesus' 'prayer requests' to the Father for those who belong to him through grace:

- That we would be kept by God (protected, watched over, undertaken for).
- That we would possess the full measure of Christ's joy within us.
- That we would be kept from the evil one throughout the time we remain in the world.
- That we would be increasingly sanctified by the word of truth.
- That all who will believe in him *will believe*.
- That ours as believers would be a blessed oneness even as the Father and Son are one.
- That we would be brought safely to heaven itself, to be with Christ and to behold his glory.

Is that enough to be going on with?!

Jesus asks necessarily, continually and effectually for us

He asks *necessarily*, because although Christians are justified sinners, yet still we are sinners—still polluted by indwelling sin, still unable of ourselves to perform any acceptable spiritual act.

He asks *continually*, 'since he always lives to make

intercession for [us]' (Hebrews 7:25). He never leaves his post, never grows weary, never leaves us on one side, not even for a moment.

And he asks *effectually*. He cannot fail. When engaged in prayer later in this chapter, Jesus will say, 'Father, I thank you that you have heard me. I knew that you always hear me' (verses 41–42). The Father will never refuse the Son. He will always hear and answer him, which leads directly to a second matter.

The Father answering the Son

Back to Martha's testimony in verse 22: 'Whatever you ask from God, God will give you.' That phrase, 'God will give you', runs deep—far deeper, maybe, than Martha yet understood. The '*will* give' is, in truth, '*must* give'. We said at the end of the previous paragraph, the Father will always hear and answer the Son. That may properly be strengthened to read, the Father *must* always hear and answer the Son, and in hearing and answering him, the Father must grant the Son's requests. But why? For what reasons? On what grounds? Again, there are four things to observe:

Because of who the Son is to the Father

Remember what the Father himself says of the Son, the one who even in eternity was daily his delight (Proverbs 8:30). What does he say of him? 'Behold my servant, whom I uphold, my chosen, in whom my soul delights …' (Isaiah 42:1). 'This is my beloved Son, with whom I am well pleased' (Matthew 3:17).

Because the will of the Father and the will of the Son is absolutely one

Jesus himself tells us so, in a verse we have already noted. 'I and the Father are one' (John 10:30). You and I, in praying for ourselves and for one another, could easily ask amiss, even when we ask with the best of motives (especially, for the glory of God). But the Son can never ask anything amiss. And godly, grieving Martha knew this and acknowledged this in what she says to Jesus here. There can never be even the slightest possible danger of the Son ever asking the Father something which was contrary to, in collision with, or in any way disputed by the Father's will. They share one identical will.

Because the Father has given to the Son 'All authority in heaven and on earth' (Matthew 28:18)

That assures us that, when interceding for us in heaven, the Son does not approach the Father weakly, timidly, cautiously, apologetically, double-mindedly, or in any such manner. Rather, he approaches mightily, confidently, powerfully, and always knowing that he will be welcomed. He approaches, not to persuade, cajole, or in some way attempt to *make* the Father willing; but rather, as our heavenly 'advocate with the Father, Jesus Christ the righteous' (1 John 2:1), to spread our case before him (the Father), knowing anyway that the Father would come to our aid.

Because the special focus of the Son's asking is the church

Why is this important? Think it through. The church is the 'apple' of the Father's eye (Deuteronomy 32:10). The church is 'the church of God, which he obtained with his own blood' (Acts 20:28, and compare Ephesians 5:25, '... Christ loved the church and gave himself up for her'). The church is the bride which the Father has chosen for his Son: 'And I saw the holy city, new Jerusalem, coming down out of heaven from God, prepared as a bride adorned for her husband' (Revelation 21:2, and compare Revelation 19:6–7, 'Hallelujah! For the Lord our God the Almighty reigns. Let us rejoice and exult and give him the glory, for the marriage of the Lamb has come, and his Bride has made herself ready').

The church is very much upon the Father's heart at all times. She is the focus of his electing, redeeming, pardoning, persevering, glorifying purposes of love and grace. The heart of the Father and Son in heaven is very much towards his people, the church on earth.

Arising out of what Martha says to Jesus are these two abiding themes: the Son asking the Father, and the Father answering the Son. And do not miss this: the 'even now'. These are words of humble faith and holy expectation. In what appeared to be the worst of extremities, the darkest of hours, the most mysterious of providences, the heaviest of griefs, '… even now', says Martha, 'I know that whatever you ask from God, God will give you.' She is persuaded that 'even now' it is not too late for Jesus to ask the Father, and for the Father to do what he asks for Lazarus and for them. What a thing it is to be known, loved, spoken of and prayed for in heaven!

Do you know this praying Lord Jesus Christ for yourself? If you do, praise him and rejoice. Let his powerful, prevailing intercession be a true comfort to you. If (as yet) you do not, he offers himself to you in the gospel to be your Saviour, Lord, Friend and so much more, including the one who prays for his own.

8

Jesus' two-edged sword

John 11:23–24

By way of approach to the next verses of John 11, pause to take in two appropriate verses of Scripture, which are related to each other.

Hebrews 4:12. 'For the word of God is living and active, sharper than any two-edged sword, piercing to the division of soul and of spirit, of joints and of marrow, and discerning the thoughts and intentions of the heart.'

Revelation 1:16. 'In his right hand he held seven stars, from his mouth came a sharp two-edged sword, and his face was like the sun shining in full strength.'

The first of the two refers to the great character and quality of Scripture to discern motives and to pass judgments, such that none of us and nothing of us is ever hidden from God's sight. The second speaks of the risen, ascended, glorified Lord Jesus Christ, and his authority and power to teach and to judge, to reckon with mankind, such that he cannot be avoided or by-passed (however much people attempt to do that very thing). Both have in common the reference to a 'two-edged sword'.

Our sight of the Saviour now before us in verses 23–24 concerns *Jesus' two-edged sword*, which we see in operation as he continues his conversation with Martha outside Bethany.

Jesus' statement to Martha

Martha has just said to the Lord, 'But even now I know that whatever you ask from God, God will give you.' Although Jesus had sent word to Mary and Martha that Lazarus' sickness would 'not lead to death', he had died, and that despite their natural and fervent longing that he would recover. Now, following on immediately from these words of Martha in verse 22, Jesus says to her: 'Your brother will rise again.'

Dwell on those few words. Jesus knew exactly what he was going to do, and when he was going to do it. In the present case he would raise dead Lazarus from the grave that very day and restore him to his loved ones. Let it be emphasised again, Jesus *knew* what he was going to do and when he was going to do it. And in uttering these words, he had in mind for the sisters and their brother immediate blessings, present joys, direct comforts and divine encouragements, there and then. He did not say what that was going to be, however—not yet. Rather, in these recorded words, he made this broad statement, this general promise, but no more. Yet he showed no anger or displeasure in what Martha had just said to him.

So how did she respond?

Martha's response to Jesus

And here is something very interesting. Notwithstanding her passionate desire to have Jesus do something straightaway for Lazarus (and having expressed herself in verse 22 with her 'even now'), yet observe what she actually does. In her reply, in verse 24, 'I know that he will rise again in the resurrection on the last day', she casts all her thoughts and hopes forward. She takes the long view of the future. And in so doing, she missed the *first edge* of Jesus' two-edged sword (all those present blessings that he was going to provide for his own glory and for the family's delight). She laid hold only of the *second edge* of that two-edged sword (the fact that Lazarus, having lately died, would 'rise again in the resurrection on the last day'). He would indeed! In saying 'I know' on this matter, Martha was absolutely correct, of course. But at this point in proceedings between herself and Jesus, she missed the sense of those blessings which were prepared for that very day, those immediate blessings, present joys, direct comforts and divine encouragements.

In dealing with Martha in this way, Jesus was not teasing her but testing her in order to see just how much she made of his words. And in so doing he brings to light and puts his kindly finger upon a weakness that we too can suffer in our Christian lives. It is this: that all too often we do not take God's word either *far enough* or *deep enough*. In this, Martha (though greatly loved by Jesus and greatly loving him) is a believer 'with a nature like ours' (James 5:17); a child of God just as we are.

This is worth exploring a little further, in three directions.

Martha set her own limits on Jesus' words

What exactly has Jesus said to her? 'Your brother will rise again.' 'Ah!', thought Martha, 'of course he will—won't we all?'

Do you see what she was doing? She concluded straightaway that Jesus did not mean anything more or anything else than that. And that is a mistake which we too can often make. We treat the word of the Lord as a much shallower thing than it is. We see an immediate, basic meaning and are satisfied with that, and just leave it there. We take it no further, we dig no deeper, we scale no higher, we meditate upon it no more fully.

The result of this is that (unintentionally, maybe) we limit God as to the manner of his own words and working. It is easy to criticise his disciples for their lack of grip at times, and the apparent ease at which they got the wrong end of the stick—just look back to verses 12–13. Yet we are often remarkably just like them. Often we resemble small children, only able to make little things out of big words.

How we need our minds to be expanded, our hearts to be uplifted, our appetites to be increased and our expectations to be enlarged, in order that we might reach something more of the heights and the depths, the excellencies and the glories, the mysteries and the beauties of God's mighty, amazing and glorious word!

Martha put Jesus' words on the shelf for another time

It is almost as if she was saying, 'Well, yes, I know that my brother will rise. I believe that. But what use is that to me right now, in my present circumstances? How is that going to help me get through today and the coming days?'

Again, do you see what she was doing? She was putting Jesus' words far into the distance, up a siding, on the shelf. If only she could have responded with a full heart, seeing in Jesus' promise to her the assurance that that very day Lazarus would be restored to her, what a rich blessing that would have been to her!

While the circumstances of the Bethany family were very particular to them, and we have no business in our day to expect the Lord to raise the dead before our very eyes, yet we can still fall into Martha's trap. How? By saying. 'I believe God's promises, but they are not for me—or, at least, not yet. I believe God's promises, but I dare not claim them for myself or plead them in prayer. I believe God's promises, but they seem somehow to be too good to be true.' So we put them to one side or push them into the future.

Here are a handful of familiar Scriptures which we might easily push into the future but have great importance *now*:

Psalm 16:8. 'I have set the LORD always before me; because he is at my right hand, I shall not be shaken.'

Isaiah 40:31. '... but they who wait for the LORD shall renew their strength; they shall mount up with wings like eagles; they shall run and not be weary; they shall walk and not faint.'

John 15:7. 'If you abide in me, and my words abide in you, ask whatever you wish, and it will be done for you.'

2 Corinthians 12:9. 'But he said to me, "My grace is sufficient for you, for my power is made perfect in weakness."'

1 John 1:7. 'But if we walk in the light, as he is in the light, we have fellowship with one another, and the blood of Jesus his Son cleanses us from all sin.'

Again and again, Jesus' words and promises are not just for tomorrow, next year, another time, or for someone else. Again and again they are for us, right now! While today is today!

And if these pages have come into your hand as someone who is yet to become a Christian, here is a verse for you as well, from the lips of Jesus.

John 8:24. 'I told you that you would die in your sins, for unless you believe that I am he you will die in your sins.'

Life rushes on. Only a little while and you will stand before God. Today—even this very moment as you read these words—there is grace, forgiveness, salvation, rest, peace, joy, eternal life, mercy, hope and much, much more to be found in 'the unsearchable riches of Christ' (Ephesians 3:8). Do not lose the treasures offered to you freely and abundantly in the gospel, because of your unbelief.

Martha made Jesus' words impersonal

The truth is that Jesus' words to Martha in verse 23 are highly personal, but she did not take them that way. Her response appears to be along the lines of, 'Yes, Lazarus will rise again in the resurrection on the last day along with everyone else.' That is absolutely true. All mankind, the entire human race, *will* arise to appear before the Lord on the day he has appointed. But still she missed the point of the personal interest which Jesus takes in each one of his own. She missed the richness of the personal support and stay which his words and the promises they contained were intended to bring to *her*, not only to his people as a whole. She missed the wonder of appreciating the blessedly familiar way in which Jesus thinks of each one of his family. She missed the fact that so often his messages come to us, as it were, in envelopes with our own name on.

Once more, this can be the mistake we all make. As a result, we can end up sitting hungry at a feast or remaining thirsty beside a flowing stream. Yet if God is your portion, your everything, your all-in-all (the Father your Shepherd, the Son your Saviour, the Holy Spirit your Sanctifier), do not fail or even hesitate to grasp with the firm hands of personal faith the royal blessings which the Lord Jesus Christ sets before you in all that he says to you in his word.

Remember the grand and glowing testimony of Joshua, nearing the end of his life. 'And now I am about to go the way of all the earth, and you know in your hearts and souls, all of you, that not one word has failed of all the good things [or, 'words'] that the LORD your God has promised concerning you. All have come to pass for you; not one of them has failed.' (Joshua 23:14.) And put beside it the urgent exhortation of the apostle Paul: 'Let the word of Christ dwell in you richly ...' (Colossians 3:16).

The Lord has so much to say to us and to grant to us *today*, just as he had for Martha *that day*. And with regard to the words and promises of the Lord that clearly are only for the future, then learn to wait patiently until their appropriate arrival and performance date, knowing that they will surely come to pass. For they come from 'God, who never lies' (Titus 1:2).

9

Jesus' glorious promise

John 11:23–24

'Today's the day!' we sometimes exclaim. We are very much creatures of days, and there are all sorts of 'days' in our lives: good days and bad days, precious days we shall remember and desperate days we would rather forget, better days and worse days. There are birthdays, wedding days, exam days, hospital appointment days, holidays, decision days, up days and down days, happy days and sad days, smooth days and difficult days, quick days and dragging days, empty days and full days, insignificant days and crunch days, fruitful days and wasted days—on and on it goes.

Staying for now with verses 23–24 of John 11, they record a unique and remarkable day. When it happens, there will never have been one like it in the past, nor will there ever be one like it following. Jesus speaks very directly and specifically of it in his words to Martha here. 'Your brother will rise again.' To which Martha (whose much-loved brother Lazarus has now been dead for four days) responds, 'I know that he will rise again in the resurrection on the last day.' And it is in those words of Jesus to Martha that we discover *Jesus' glorious promise.*

We noticed earlier that these words he spoke were two-edged. Jesus had in mind, first of all, what he was going to do *that very day* (perform his mighty miracle of raising Lazarus, commanding him to come out of the burial tomb, and restore him alive and well to his two sisters). Martha, however, as we saw, missed that edge of his sword, and went straight to the second edge (the general resurrection of all mankind 'on the last day'). What she said, of course, is absolutely true, but what Jesus would do *that latter day* was only part of what he was saying. It is, however, to *this* part that we now give our focus.

It is a plain (and regrettable) fact that all people pay far too little attention to the prospect of this day—when, that is, they pay any attention to it at all. It is also a plain (and regrettable) fact that, by and large, Christians pay far too little attention to it as well. Yet this rising again, this 'resurrection on the last day' is the day which no one can escape.

Let us ask and seek to answer four leading questions concerning it.

Who will rise?

In a word, everyone! All who have ever lived, from the very beginning of creation. The entire human race will be there, with none missing. Everyone will be personally involved and among those present on the resurrection day. There will be no exceptions or apologies for absence.

Those who have died prior to that day and are in their graves will come out of them. Their bodies will be raised up whenever or wherever they died (on the land, on the sea or in the air).

Those who are still alive on that day here on the earth will not suddenly die and be raised to life again. Rather, such a change will suddenly come to pass upon them, that instead of dying and rising again, their bodies will become like those bodies which *have been* raised from their graves. The apostle Paul speaks of this in 1 Corinthians 15:51 and the verses following. He begins in this way. 'Behold! I tell you a mystery. We shall not all sleep [that is, have died—remember the image Jesus used of Lazarus in John 11:11], but we shall all be changed, in a moment, in the twinkling of an eye, at the last trumpet.'

What an assembly it will be. Every man and woman, boy and girl who has ever lived, every believer and every unbeliever. How can you count the countless or number the innumerable? All the teeming millions from across the globe with all its nations will be there. All will rise. All will be there.

We must not make the mistake of thinking of this merely in the *general.* It will all be highly *personal.* You and I will be there: I who write these words, and you who read them. I will rise again. You will rise again. We shall each of us stand there in our appointed place, before 'the judgment seat of Christ' (2 Corinthians 5:10), which is 'the judgment seat of God' (Romans 14:10).

When will we rise?

When will this resurrection be? Verse 24 states 'on the last day'. It is important to distinguish between the last *days* and the last *day.* We are actually living through what Scripture calls 'the last days'. An example of such a reference is 2 Timothy 3:1, where the veteran Paul writes to the much younger Timothy, 'But understand this, that in the last days there will come times of difficulty.' The phrase refers to the entire period between the first and second comings of the Lord Jesus Christ. The last day, on the other hand, will come at the very end of the last days. Jesus speaks of it in John 6:39–40. In the first of these two verses, for example, he says: 'And this is the will of him who sent me, that I should lose nothing of all that he has given me, but raise it up on the last day.'

The day will dawn. The hour will strike. The timing of it (of which we are not told and are not to speculate) will be in connection with the second coming of Jesus. That might be still hundreds of years off, or it might be much sooner than anyone thinks at any time. Either way, we are to consider it as near. 'You also, be patient. Establish your hearts, for the coming of the Lord is at hand. … the Judge is standing at the door.' (James 5:8–9.) In one of his messages recorded in the Acts of the Apostles, Paul declares, God '… commands all people everywhere to repent, because he has fixed a day on which he will judge the world in righteousness by a man whom he has appointed; and of this he has given assurance to all by raising him from the dead' (Acts 17:30–31). Notice there how the resurrection of Jesus is used by Paul as a guarantee of the resurrection of all people at the end of the present age.

Who will raise us?

Shall we do it ourselves? Never! This will be the work of God. He it is who raises the dead, just as he it was who raised his Son. 'With man it is impossible, but not with God. For all things are possible with God,' says Jesus (Mark 10:27). Cannot the great creator God, who made all things out of nothing at the very beginning, raise men's bodies after they have died, even after they have been dead for centuries? Cannot he distinguish one person's dust or remains from another's? Is he liable to make any mistakes about his own creatures? Cannot he, in whom is joined infinite understanding (omniscience) and infinite power (omnipotence), and who can subdue all things to himself, perform this mighty work?

You and I cannot grasp this. It is beyond our limited abilities fully to imagine or take in, but we must not go on from there to doubt or question it. It is entirely in the hands of God. How very small a portion do we yet know of his ways. 'Why is it thought incredible by any of you that God raises the dead?' (Acts 26:8).

To what shall we rise?

Listen to the united testimony of Scripture:

Daniel 12:2. 'And many of those who sleep in the dust of the earth shall awake, some to everlasting life, and some to shame and everlasting contempt.'

John 5:28–29. 'Do not marvel at this, for an hour is coming when all who are in the tombs will hear his voice and come out, those who have done good to the resurrection of life, and those who have done evil to the resurrection of judgment.'

We are being brought face to face here with the twin solemn realities of heaven and hell. Just as there is a vast difference between the godly and the ungodly in their life and in their death, so it will be also in the resurrection. In between the two (between death and resurrection) there is no place for repentance, no provision of forgiveness, no possibility of reformation, no proclamation of salvation. *Everything is settled at death.*

If you die saved (trusting in Jesus as your Saviour), you

will rise saved. If you die unbelieving (rejecting Jesus as your Saviour), you will rise unbelieving. If you die holy (washed, cleansed and sanctified), you will rise holy. If you die unclean (still in your sins), you will rise unclean. *It is as stark as that.* Please do not let any false teachers persuade you otherwise.

When the John 5 verses just quoted speak of those who have 'done good' and those who have 'done evil', do not misunderstand what Jesus is saying. This verse is not intended to give the impression that salvation is in our own hands or in any way dependent upon our own works. Salvation is all of grace. A vital verse on this is Ephesians 2:5: '… by grace you have been saved'. This is amplified moments later in verses 8–9: 'For by grace you have been saved through faith. And this is not your own doing; it is the gift of God, not a result of works, so that no one may boast.'

So 'those who have done good', back in John 5, refers to those who, having been saved by grace (by the undeserved mercy of God, when in truth we deserved the very opposite of mercy, namely condemnation), are trusting in Christ, fearing God, loving his commandments, and honouring his name. They will rise 'to the resurrection of life'. They will come forth from their graves to inexpressible joy and blessing. The reunion of their souls and bodies will be an embrace of pure delight, to the glory of God. But 'those who have done evil' refers to those who, having spurned repeatedly God's offers of grace and turned a deaf ear to all his overtures of mercy, have cared nothing or little for his name and commandments, taken their own course and gone their own way. They will rise 'to the resurrection of judgment'. They will come forth from their graves to inexpressible shame and misery. The reunion of their souls and bodies will be a most wretched and unwelcome embrace. Hence Jesus' extremely solemn words at the end of one of his parables, when he speaks of those who 'will go away into eternal punishment' and 'the righteous into eternal life' (Matthew 25:46).

Are you prepared for the last day? Our families and friends will say their farewells to us as they lay us in our graves and leave us there. But God will not leave us there. We each and all have a fixed appointment to appear before him. Are you ready for that?

10

Jesus' staggering claim

John 11:25–26

All sorts of people have made and do make all sorts of claims for themselves: who they are, what they can do, what they have accomplished, and so on. Records are kept of who is the oldest, tallest, richest, strongest, cleverest, fastest and much else besides. People are constantly in competition with one another, in the hope of coming out on top and staying there.

But the claims made for himself by the Lord Jesus Christ are in a class by themselves. *They stand alone, because he stands alone.*

Among these various claims made by Jesus, none perhaps are better known than his 'I am' sayings; seven separate occasions, all recorded in John's gospel, concerning his own person and work, with each of them beginning with the words 'I am'. It is very important to note that this very manner of speaking is a testimony to Jesus' deity, to him being God. The grounds for this statement? They are found way back in Exodus 3:14, where God, in commissioning Moses for the great task ahead of him, reveals himself to Moses as 'I AM WHO I AM'. It is the self-revelation of the everlasting God. And Jesus takes such words to himself, including in the verses of John 11:25–26 here. This is what Jesus says of himself to Martha: 'I am the resurrection and the life.' Here is a statement which has great depths to it so that, like a mighty ocean, we cannot see its bottom. Consider *Jesus' staggering claim*:

Jesus' claim concerning himself

Indeed, to say, 'I am the resurrection and the life', is a staggering claim—it seems, if anything, an understatement. To 'staggering', we could add startling, amazing, extraordinary. What exactly is Jesus saying? At least three things stand out:

Jesus is affirming that he himself is God

This is against the background, mentioned above, of the language of Exodus 3:14. Follow the logic. Since 'I am' is the divine name, and Jesus uses it of himself, he is of necessity making a claim to his own deity. No one could make this claim except one who is God. And, of course, the Lord Jesus Christ is exactly that: he is God (how ever many people then and now dispute that truth). Jesus is spoken of in John 1:14 in this way: 'And the Word became flesh and dwelt among us …'. He is the one who 'came down from heaven' (John 6:41). He is God 'manifested in the flesh' (1 Timothy 3:16). When asked at his trial by the high priest, 'Are you the Christ, the Son of the Blessed?', Jesus replied, 'I am', adding 'and you will see the Son of Man seated at the right hand of Power, and coming with the clouds of heaven' (Mark 14:61–62). Clearly the high priest understood what Jesus was claiming for himself, and immediately charged him with 'blasphemy' (Mark 14:64).

So let us be in no doubt that here in John 11, in speaking to

Martha, Jesus is affirming that he himself is God. Martha was standing in the divine presence of the one who speaks of the divine name and rightly takes it to himself.

Jesus is affirming that the full blessed life of God is found in him

In other words, these are not mere words. They declare that all the glorious divine attributes belong to him. 'For in him the whole fullness of deity dwells bodily' (Colossians 2:9). A rich array of these attributes is on display here in the course of John 11. These include his omnipotence, omniscience, love, compassion, power, wisdom, holiness and the list goes on. Take a moment to search out as many as you can, just from this one chapter.

Jesus is affirming that he is himself the Lord and Giver of life

He is the ever-living one. He has life in himself. His is 'the power of an indestructible life' (Hebrews 7:16). He is the source, the fountain, the very Lord of life. In him is life. *He gives life to dead sinners*, that believing upon him we pass 'from death to life …' (John 5:24), from being dead in sin to being made alive in Jesus. 'For this is the will of my Father', Jesus says, 'that everyone who looks on the Son and believes in him should have eternal life' (John 6:40). *He gives life to new-born Christians*: the life of grace, faith, holiness, obedience and 'joy and peace in believing' (Romans 15:13), as he continues to work by the Holy Spirit. *He gives life that lasts for ever*, promising for all who are his that 'I will raise him up on the last day' (John 6:44). How so? He has dealt with sin (by his death), conquered death and won a great victory over the grave (by his resurrection), and is preparing heaven for us (by his ascension and coronation). There is no spiritual life apart from the Lord Jesus Christ, but in him there is life in all its fullness and abundance (John 10:10).

These words of Jesus, 'I am the resurrection and the life', demand our attention and defy our unbelief. So they should.

Jesus' claim concerning those who believe in him

This second truth follows on directly and intimately from the first. Straight after 'I am the resurrection and the life' (verse 25a) come two statements which are companions of one another: 'Whoever believes in me, though he die, yet shall he live' (verse 25b); 'and everyone who lives and believes in me shall never die' (verse 26a). Each has its own emphasis, and there is no contradiction between them. In speaking as he does to Martha, Jesus is doing something wonderfully tender, kind and gracious.

Martha is still taken up with her dead brother Lazarus, understandably. Jesus, however, would rather have her taken up with himself, so he seeks to instruct her. Observe the loving manner in which he does this. Lazarus is her brother, but he, Jesus, is her Saviour, and so he is the one of whom she needs a fresh sight. We need exactly the same, and we need to feel the truth and power of what he says here. We need to 'grow in the grace and knowledge of our Lord and Saviour Jesus Christ' (2 Peter 3:18); both are essential, the 'grace' *and* the 'knowledge'.

What, then, is the claim Jesus makes here for all those who are believing and trusting in him? What are these twin companion truths?

We shall live, even though we die

Lazarus had been alive and now had died. It is a common story, happening every moment of every day. Life and death never cease. While I have been writing this chapter, countless people will have died and passed into eternity. It should be a most solemn thought because it will be the same for each one of us. Christians are not somehow miraculously immune from that.

But—and what a 'but' it is!—what happens to those who die believing in Jesus as their precious Saviour and glorious Lord? In the fullest sense we can possibly give to Jesus' words here, we live, we are alive! 'Whoever believes in me, though he die, yet shall he live.' Is death the end of the life of trusting and believing? No! What is, then? Life!

This is not a riddle, it is a fact. Life *in Christ* on earth is exchanged for life *with Christ* in heaven. This is surely the very heart of the apostle Paul's famous testimony: 'For to me to live is Christ, and to die is gain' (Philippians 1:21). Or (as we try to capture the particular focus of his words): to live—Christ; to die—more Christ! Two verses later he leaves us in no doubt: 'My desire is to depart and be with Christ, for that is far better' (Philippians 1:23b).

We shall never die

Feel the force of Jesus' words here. After having just said 'though he die, yet shall he live', Jesus adds the key word *never*: 'everyone who lives and believes in me shall never die'. The full impact of that 'never' is 'never ever' or 'by no means ever'. This life ends at whatever age any believer is at the time of death. The body is laid in the grave; physical death cannot be escaped. But physical death, however it is met, cannot quench the Christian's true life. Indeed, a fundamental part of the reason why for the Christian death is gain, is that it introduces us to the full enjoyment of life. It is customary to speak of this present life as the land of the living, and that what follows after it is the land of the dying. Yet for the Christian this is emphatically the wrong way round. Here, we are in the land of the dying; then, when we die, we go to the land of the living.

Jesus' claim demanding our response

The statement of Jesus we are looking at has not quite finished. He asks a highly personal question at the end of verse 26, first to Martha (face to face), and now to all of us. 'Do you believe this?' In other words, does what Jesus has just been saying have the ring of truth to your soul? Jesus has made this staggering claim. Do you believe him?

This is a question posed to every unbeliever

The unbeliever, because he is an unbeliever, rejects it all. It is the very nature of unbelief to dispute every claim Jesus makes, every word he speaks. The unbeliever would mock the gospel and call the Son of God a liar. It is by faith that these truths are grasped, faith in the Lord Jesus Christ, believing him, believing upon him. And faith and unbelief are opposites.

This is a question posed to every believer

The believer, however, still has to face Jesus' question here. He brings it right home. Christian: do *you* believe every word of Jesus, including the claim he makes here? Are his words in verses 25–26 your personal assurance concerning your own eternal position and standing? Are they your comfort when you mourn the passing of even your dearest loved ones who die in the Lord?

This is a question posed to everyone

In order to be as clear as possible, for we are dealing with eternal issues here: is the Lord Jesus Christ Lord of *your* life? Paul speaks for all true believers when he writes, 'When Christ who is your life appears, then you also will appear with him in glory' (Colossians 3:4). Jesus is only the 'life' of those who trust him as their Saviour and follow him as their Lord, those who regard him as the sole and sufficient ground for themselves as poor and needy sinners to come to God and be reconciled to him for ever.

Do you know what it is to belong to the great 'I am'? Make sure, in your reply, that you realise the eternal significance of what you say.

11

Jesus' direct question

John 11:26–27

A question which it is well for each and every one of us to ask is, 'Am I a true believer, a real Christian?' This is the most important question we can ever ask, for no room must be allowed for self-deceit, lest we be hypocrites now and castaways at the last. Those two words in the question, believer and Christian, are interchangeable. It is the first of them, however, that the Lord Jesus focuses upon in his conversation with Martha.

Having made his staggering 'I am' claim, he looks Martha in the eye and asks her what we may call *Jesus' direct question*: 'Do you believe this?' (end of verse 26). His claim was not delivered to her in a 'take it or leave it' manner. It required, indeed demanded, a personal response. It still does, for the question put to Martha by Jesus is the question he puts to each of us.

Can you see straightaway what Jesus is doing here with Martha? He is pressing her on the matter of personal faith, personal belief, in himself. 'Do you believe in me? Do you accept my claim? Do you acknowledge what I say? Do you embrace my words? Am I the one I say I am?' This, and more, lies behind and within his question, 'Do you believe this?' And the 'believe' is no mere intellectual assent—it is far more than that. It is the personal laying hold through faith, not only of the words that have been spoken but of the one who has spoken them.

Three things are here for us to take careful notice of:

The firmness of faith

Martha gives an immediate response to Jesus' question: 'Yes, Lord; I believe' (verse 27). Of the two sisters, Martha and Mary, some folk have tended to have something of a 'down' on Martha. Maybe this arises from a false understanding of the episode recorded at the end of Luke 10, where Mary 'sat at the Lord's feet and listened to his teaching' (verse 39), while Martha 'was distracted with much serving' (verse 40), being busy in the kitchen. What Martha's detractors miss, however, is that she was engaged in her domestic tasks for the glory of the Lord Jesus, the honoured guest in their home.

What has this to do with the verses we are considering here? Some have taken it upon themselves to pronounce that Martha did not really answer Jesus' question, in relation to what he had just said about 'the resurrection and the life'. What she did (they insist) is that she fell back on a vaguer and more general statement of belief, and that later on in the chapter (verse 39) she looked to be wavering and wobbling somewhat. We should not follow this assessment.

Interestingly, her 'I believe' is literally 'I have believed'. She is declaring her positive, settled conviction about which she was not entertaining any doubts. In stark contrast to those just mentioned who would limit the genuineness of her words, there are others (rightly) who rank her testimony with some of the other classic testimonies in John's gospel concerning faith in Jesus. Here are a few examples of these: 'Behold, the Lamb of God, who takes away the sin of the world!' (John the Baptist in 1:29.) 'We have found the Messiah' (Andrew in 1:41). 'Rabbi, you are the Son of God! You are the King of Israel!' (Nathanael in 1:49.) Not forgetting the Samaritans, who declared of Jesus to the woman Jesus had met at the well, 'It is no longer because of what you said that we believe, for we have heard for ourselves, and we know that this is indeed the Saviour of the world' (4:42). And then there is Thomas, with his matchless 'My Lord and my God!' (20:28).

With regard to this word *firmness*—the *firmness of faith*—I am thinking of how true faith, true believing in Jesus, is pictured in the Scriptures as involving the whole of our being: mind, heart and will. With our *minds*, we are persuaded of the truth concerning God in Christ. With our *hearts*, we are gripped in a personal way with our need of Jesus to be our Saviour from sin, and are brought to trust and love him as such. With our *wills*, we desire to be his and his alone, absolutely belonging and totally committed.

The focus of faith

It is the Lord Jesus Christ who puts the question to Martha, and in her reply she focuses on him and is taken up with him. Maybe she did not as yet understand every possible depth and glory of the words she used, but then which of us does, since there is so much of Jesus' person and work which is still beyond our comprehension? But look at what she *does* say. With

Jesus' words about him being 'the resurrection and the life' still ringing in her ears, she freely and wholeheartedly confesses her belief that Jesus is 'the Christ, the Son of God, who is coming into the world [literally, 'the one coming into the world'].'

To say that he is 'the Christ' confesses his Messiahship, that he is the anointed one. To say that he is 'the Son of God' confesses his deity, that he is God. That he is the one 'who is coming into the world' confesses that he is the promised one, that he is himself the fulfilment of all the prophecies in the Old Testament concerning the Redeemer who would come from heaven. Martha's confession is a fulsome and an all-round statement of true faith, the entire focus of which is upon Jesus.

She is fastened upon Jesus with all her heart. So it must always be if we are *true* believers, *true* Christians. We are not to be taken up with thoughts, systems, philosophies, ideas or researches. We are not to be placing our reliance upon externals, however important they may be in their place (not least, keeping the Lord's Day, going to church, singing God's praise, listening to preaching, witnessing for Christ). We are not to be making decisions in our own wisdom or strength. If we imagine these things are the marks, the evidences, the assurances, of true faith, we need to have our false bubbles burst, our false confidences removed, our false assurances shaken: even our 'false conversions' abandoned, if need be.

Attention has been drawn to the obvious in the spelling of *faith: F*orsaking *a*ll, *I t*ake *h*im. The Lord Jesus Christ and he alone is the focus of faith. In this connection, remember the wonderful instance recorded in Acts 16 of the conversion of the Philippian jailer. In answer to his question to Paul and Silas (the greatest question that can ever be asked), 'Sirs, what must I do to be saved?', they replied (and this is the greatest answer that can ever be given), 'Believe in the Lord Jesus, and you will be saved, you and your household' (Acts 16:30–31).

It is also important to remember that in the Scriptures *true faith* always goes hand in hand with *true repentance*. This is the door with two hinges, the coin with two faces. Jesus' very first message recorded in Mark's gospel, at the commencement of his public ministry, was exactly this: 'repent and believe' (Mark 1:15). It involves sorrowing over sin and sighing after Christ; turning from sin and trusting in Christ.

The fountain of faith

The question might arise: how did Martha believe? Where did she get such faith from? To be more personal, how may we have it? Where can we get it?

The answer concerning Martha is this: God gave it to her. That is always the way. *She* believed, but the faith by which she believed was 'the gift of God'. That is what faith is, every time. Paul sets it out for us in this way: 'For by grace you have been saved through faith. And this is not your own doing; it is the gift of God, not a result of works, so that no one may boast' (Ephesians 2:8–9).

God is himself the fountain of faith. So the answer concerning us is the same as it was for Martha. Faith is God's gift—if you do not yet possess it, then you must go to God for it. Or, if you do already possess this gift of God but desire an increase of it, then, again, you must go to God, the fountain of faith. Go with the words of Jesus' apostles: 'Increase our faith' (Luke 17:5)! Go with the words of the father of the child who had an unclean spirit: 'I believe; help my unbelief' (Mark 9:24)!

God delights to be sought and asked. To do so glorifies him, for it acknowledges that he alone can help us, he alone can do us any good. Acknowledge your entire dependence upon him. Humble yourself entirely before him. Realise that you are nothing and that he is everything.

Jesus asked Martha, 'Do you believe this?' Martha replied to Jesus, 'Yes, Lord; I believe.' So before we move on, let us examine ourselves, whoever is reading these lines. How do you and I respond to Jesus' question here? What do you and I say?

- To say 'Yes' to Jesus requires a *personal* response: we must answer for ourselves.
- To say 'Yes' to Jesus requires a *thoughtful* response, thinking carefully what we say.
- To say 'Yes' to Jesus requires a *complete* response, holding nothing of ourselves back.
- To say 'Yes' to Jesus requires a *sincere* response, not just saying something for the sake of it.
- To say 'Yes' to Jesus requires a *humble* response, not imagining that we are doing God some kind of favour.
- To say 'Yes' to Jesus requires a *lasting* response, for this is not something just for the moment.
- To say 'Yes' to Jesus requires a *secure* response, one which will not only serve for this present life, but will enable you to face death comfortably, the day of judgment confidently, and that will land you safely in heaven.
- To say 'Yes' to Jesus requires a *Jesus is all* response, for nothing less and nothing else will do.

12

Jesus' tender enquiry

John 11:28–32

There is no one in all the world to compare with the Lord Jesus Christ. To those who believe upon him, know him and trust him, he is indescribably precious, lovely and all-sufficient. Sadly, it remains the case with many, many others that they find no beauty or attractiveness in him whatsoever, 'no form or majesty that [they] should look at him, and no beauty that (they) should desire him' (Isaiah 53:2). But someone to whom Jesus was 'altogether desirable' (Song of Songs 5:16) was Mary of Bethany, sister of Martha and Lazarus.

So far, Martha is the one of the two sisters who has been in the picture with Jesus. Back in verse 20 we were told, 'when Martha heard that Jesus was coming, she went and met him, but Mary remained seated in the house'. Now, however, Mary's moment has come. Martha 'went and called her sister Mary, saying in private, "The Teacher is here and is calling for you"' (verse 28). Mary's response was immediate. 'And when she heard it, she rose quickly and went to him' (verse 29). It is Jesus' message here via Martha for Mary which is what I have in mind with the phrase, *Jesus' tender enquiry*.

The name Jesus bears

The Bible is full of Jesus and the many names and titles belonging to him. You can put together more or less an entire A-Z of these names and titles. The one which Martha uses here in conveying the message to Mary is 'The Teacher'. It is a most appropriate name for him, and there is much in it. We may isolate four threads.

The thread of Jesus' authority

At the end of Jesus' sermon on the mount, it is recorded: 'And when Jesus finished these sayings, the crowds were astonished at his teaching, for he was teaching them as one who had authority, and not as their scribes' (Matthew 7:28–29). Following one of his skirmishes with the Sadducees, '... some of the scribes answered, "Teacher, you have spoken well." For they no longer dared to ask him any question.' (Luke 20:39–40.) In John 7:46, the officers who had been sent by the chief priests and Pharisees to arrest Jesus, returned saying of him, 'No one ever spoke like this man'.

The thread of Jesus being the fount of all wisdom

Paul asserts of Jesus, 'in whom are hidden all the treasures of wisdom and knowledge' (Colossians 2:3), while John 2:25 affirms that Jesus 'needed no one to bear witness about man, for he himself knew what was in man'!

The thread of Jesus' captivating influence

For all that Jesus faced many opponents throughout his ministry, there were times when 'the great throng heard him gladly' (Mark 12:37), and when 'many followed him' (Matthew 12:15).

The thread of Jesus as the Head, Governor and Ruler of his people, the church

As such, he says to us, 'If you abide in my word, you are truly my disciples, and you will know the truth, and the truth will set you free' (John 8:31–32). He tells his disciples, 'The words that I have spoken to you are spirit and life' (John 6:63b), and we are bidden by the apostle Paul to 'Let the word of Christ dwell in [us] richly ...' (Colossians 3:16).

This title, 'Teacher', is a name which appears again and again in the gospels pertaining to Jesus. How we need to ensure that he is *our* Teacher, that we belong to him, that every thought and longing of ours is brought into captivity to him, and that, like Mary in Luke 10 (mentioned in the previous section), we are continually sitting at his feet and listening to his teaching.

He is no ordinary teacher, not one in a line of teachers. He stands alone in this, as he does in everything. In this, he is filled with both majesty and sweetness which raises him above all other men, like some mountainous peak which rises above all the smaller hills. He is *the* Teacher. Is he yours?

The desire Jesus expresses

This message from Jesus for Mary is very simple and very personal. In every sense it has Mary's name written upon it, and no one else's. Moreover, Martha did not call it out across the room in the house for everyone to hear. Rather, she spoke to Mary 'in private', and no doubt in a subdued tone.

Several most worthwhile things are here for us to meditate upon in the Teacher 'calling for' Mary:

The Lord Jesus Christ delights in the fellowship of his people

Think it through: to Jesus, as the Son of God, there belongs within the Godhead fellowship with both the Father and the Holy Spirit. Each person delights in the other. Yet (speaking carefully here), notwithstanding that, his heart is filled especially with strong desires for his people, for *our* company and fellowship. Knowing our own hearts as we need to do, we genuinely wonder sometimes why this should be so—why he should be desirous of us in this way and what possible pleasure our company can really give him. But the fact remains! It is intensely moving to read of Jesus saying to his disciples at the last supper, 'I have earnestly desired to eat this Passover with you before I suffer' (Luke 22:15); and then, not long before his betrayal and arrest, 'You are those who have stayed with me in my trials' (Luke 22:28).

If you should ask how or where Jesus meets and fellowships in a special way with us, then the answer is twofold: in his word and at his table, in both of which he calls for us and comes to us.

The Lord Jesus Christ delights to enquire for us

Jesus was here 'calling for' Mary, not just in the sense of summoning her to come and meet him, but in some sense also of being greatly, tenderly, affectionately and personally concerned for her, knowing all about her sadness and troubled circumstances. And such is still his continual attitude towards each and every one of his disciples, both then and now.

He would press upon us at these times such questions as these: How is it with your soul? What do you think of me? How much do you desire me? Do you love me? He is not content just to let us drift along in our Christian lives and experience, but would prompt us for our spiritual health and our spiritual good. In this, his ministry to us as 'Teacher' is combined with his ministry to us as 'Physician'.

Once again, if you should ask as to how or where in particular he calls for us and comes to us, then the answer is twofold: in his word and at his table.

The Lord Jesus Christ delights to take a highly personal and intimate interest in us

He had just spent time with Martha. This had been exclusive time, with and for her alone. It was also patient and precious time. Now it is Mary's turn for Jesus to do the same with her. Jesus is 'calling [or, asking] for *you*', Martha tells Mary.

We mentioned above that Martha did not make any song or dance about this; it was done 'in private'. The word used here can carry the sense of 'quietly' or' 'secretly'. We can imagine Martha speaking in a whisper. There were visitors in the Bethany home (remember verse 19), and it was not for them that Jesus had sent a message. It was just for Mary.

This is true to Jesus' regular manner. Many are the instances recorded in the gospels of individual and personal encounters of Jesus with different people, as well as with his disciples as a group. 'Come away by yourselves to a desolate place and rest a while,' he said to them (Mark 6:31). Speaking to his church, Jesus says, 'Behold, I stand at the door and knock. If anyone hears my voice and opens the door, I will come in to him and eat with him, and he with me.' (Revelation 3:20.) And never forget Psalm 25:14: 'The friendship [or, secret counsel] of the LORD is for those who fear him, and he makes known to them his covenant.' The place of prayer is vital and central to this for us.

The response Jesus draws

In one word: magnetic! It is a beautiful sight: 'And when she heard it, she rose quickly and went to him' (verse 29). Just as at the beginning, in verse 3, the sisters had not mentioned Lazarus by name to Jesus, just 'he whom you love', knowing that Jesus would know very well who they meant, so here in verse 28 Martha had not mentioned Jesus by name to Mary, just 'The Teacher', knowing that Mary would know very well who she meant, and she did. That one name, 'Teacher', was quite enough to identify the Lord Jesus, the one who was 'distinguished among ten thousand' (Song of Songs 5:10) to Mary's soul. The words, 'The Teacher', conveyed to Mary the force of '*my* Teacher'. She had only one, and he had come at last.

When she came to Jesus (who was still outside Bethany and had not yet entered the village or the home), Mary spoke the same words as Martha had spoken to him earlier. 'Lord, if you had been here, my brother would not have died' (verse 32b). Yet there is a highly significant difference from the occasion with her sister. Note it carefully. 'Now when Mary came to where Jesus was and saw him, she fell at his feet …' Mary loved to be at Jesus' feet (remember Luke 10:39 once more, and add John 12:3 as another example). In adopting this position before him, she was exalting him in adoring worship and bowing before him in humble submission. Taking these three instances together, it has been suggested that in Luke 10, in listening to Jesus' teaching, Mary was honouring him as her Prophet. In John 11, in bringing to him her sorrows, she was honouring him as her Priest. In John 12, in pouring expensive ointment on his feet, she was honouring him as her King. Prophet, Priest and King are what we refer to as the three offices of Christ.

Do you and I regard the Lord Jesus Christ as Mary regarded him? Do we do so with the same adoration, submission and devotion? Is our response the same as hers at the thought of 'The Teacher', at the sound of his voice, at the mention of his name?

Let us finish this section with these questions for our self-examination. I'll express them in a personal manner to each one reading these lines.

- Upon whom do you lavish your worship?
- To whom do you pour out your soul and go with all your troubles and perplexities?
- To whose voice do you give your undivided attention?
- To whom is your life devoted in wholehearted service and continual praise?
- To the 'Teacher'? To the one whom Mary knew?

We end this section as we began it. There is no one in all the world to compare with the Lord Jesus Christ. Have you made that discovery yet? If you have, are you discovering more and more each day? If you have not, would you make that discovery now?

13

Jesus' flowing tears

John 11:33-36

The oldest person who ever lived? Methuselah, aged 969 when he died (Genesis 5:27).

The longest psalm in the Bible? Psalm 119, with 176 verses.

The shortest Bible verse? John 11:35 (just two words, 'Jesus wept'; three words in Greek, incorporating a definite article which remains untranslated in English). Yes, the shortest verse in Scripture, but how very full it is! And it is this verse which is at the very heart of the section of John 11 to which we now turn, verses 33–36. We are on holy ground as we consider *Jesus' flowing tears.*

Jesus' tears show us what a real and true man he is

We must never be in any doubt about Jesus' deity/divinity, that he is God. Equally, we must never be in any doubt about his manhood/humanity, that he is man. Not partly God and partly man, in some sort of proportion, but altogether God and altogether man, having taken manhood upon himself at his incarnation, without at all ceasing to be God. In other words, he has two natures in his one person, a matter described theologically as the 'hypostatic union'. If we are to have any proper grasp of who the Lord Jesus Christ really is, we must understand this and hold firmly to it, against all opponents and deniers of it.

One of the mistakes which can be made over Jesus' manhood is, in one way or another, to water it down. Never water it down! He became one of us, bone of our bone and flesh of our flesh. He even 'in every respect has been tempted as we are' but with this one essential caveat, 'yet without sin' (Hebrews 4:15).

The moving and revealing statement that 'Jesus wept' confirms and underscores this true manhood, and fits along with other assertions in the gospels which tell us that he was hungry, thirsty, weary, disappointed, lonely, dependent upon the Father, and so on. Surely he is the 'Man of men', indeed the manliest man there has ever been. And should you ever be minded to suggest that it is somehow *un*manly for Jesus to weep (and don't be!), the truth is that it shows that he was subject to all *sinless* human emotions.

Jesus' tears show us the depths of sorrow that he felt

These few verses of John 11 include an abundance of weeping. Mary was weeping ('When Jesus saw her weeping …'). Others present were weeping ('and the Jews who had come with her also weeping'). And what do we read next concerning the Lord Jesus? That 'he was deeply moved in his spirit and greatly troubled'; and then come the famous words, 'Jesus wept'.

The emotions here recorded of Jesus need careful noting.

First, 'he was deeply moved in his [or, 'the'] spirit.' How are we to understand it? As we might expect, different people have interpreted it in different ways. From other uses of the verb, the essence of it would appear to be a combination of indignation and sympathy. Indignant, even angry (the verb has been rendered 'groaned in the spirit'), because in the death of Lazarus Jesus is face to face with the miserable ravages and effects of sin. Remember Romans 5:12: '... just as sin came into the world through one man [Adam], and death through sin, and so death spread to all men because all sinned ...'. Overflowing with sympathy, because the one who had died was one of his special friends (look back to verse 3), one whom he loved and who loved him; and because of the intense grief which Lazarus' passing had caused the precious little family in Bethany, tearing their hearts apart. In other words, in their bereavement Jesus was himself bereaved.

This is followed by 'and greatly troubled' (literally, 'troubled/ shook himself'; it may also be rendered 'was agitated' and suggests an inward disturbance). This is especially striking in view of the fact that he knew perfectly well that very shortly the overwhelming sorrow of the sisters at Bethany would be turned into overwhelming joy when he raised Lazarus from his grave. Then Jesus would give them 'the oil of gladness instead of mourning' and 'the garment of praise instead of a faint spirit' (Isaiah 61:3). He is the mourner's comforter, with nothing holding him back from this very ample demonstration of fellow-sympathy towards these people who were so dear to him.

Then, after Jesus' question, 'Where have you laid him?', and the reply, 'Lord, come and see', comes this remarkable statement, 'Jesus wept' (carrying the full force of 'Jesus burst into tears'). This was no little tear running down his cheek. No!

He wept freely: he shed abundant tears; they flowed without restraint. And Jesus was not in any way ashamed that this should be so, and be seen to be so in public.

Jesus' tears show us just how much he loves his own

The Jews (in verse 36) had it exactly right when they said, 'See how he loved him!'—even though in the very next verse, '… some of them said, "Could not he who opened the eyes of the blind man also have kept this man from dying?"'—holding his tears against him.

Jesus' tears were tears of deepest love. Love prompted him to weep. We search the Scriptures in vain for a single example of Jesus weeping for himself, weeping over his pains, sufferings and scourgings, weeping even over his sense of forsakenness when he cried out to the Father from the cross, 'My God, my God, why have you forsaken me?' (Matthew 27:46). But for love's sake, his love for his own, 'Jesus wept'. This is the only occasion where this verb occurs (the other weeping references here being a different verb). Truly, he makes his people's sorrows his own. This is the love which enables every true believer to call him 'the Son of God, who loved me and gave himself for me' (Galatians 2:20). He is the sinner's weeping Saviour and the sinner's weeping Friend.

In Luke 19:41 we find another gracious example of the Redeemer's tears, when we find him weeping over impenitent Jerusalem, whose people were utterly careless of the judgment coming upon them. And be sure to take due note of Hebrews 5:7, where we read: 'In the days of his flesh, Jesus offered up prayers and supplications, with loud cries and tears …', as he spoke to the Father.

Jesus' tears show us what a glorious one we have to take and tell our troubles to

We bring our troubles to one who is wonderfully able to feel sorrow, one who knows what it is to shed tears, one who, in this matchless passage, is in no way 'unable to sympathize with our weaknesses' (Hebrews 4:15).

Is there comfort to compare with this to be found anywhere else or in anyone else? Once again, Jesus stands completely alone. The assurance of his sympathy and tenderness towards us, his fellow-feeling with us, is not only in deeds, not only in deeds and words, but in deeds and words *and tears.* His tears here in Bethany were not pretend tears, feigned tears, crocodile tears. They were actual tears, and abundant actual tears. Because *he* wept, we may be sure that he can soothe and wipe away *our* tears. What a precious sight this must have been, and what a precious truth it contains for us. He has not changed. Now in heaven, he has not altered in any way. His heart is ever the same. 'Let us then with confidence draw near to the throne of grace, that we may receive mercy and find grace to help in time of need' (Hebrews 4:16).

Jesus' tears show us what a needful and blessed thing it is for us to weep

Are you inclined to respond, 'I don't weep, you won't catch me weeping, and certainly not in front of anyone'? Then, dear reader, I say to you, forget your proud and foolish boasting. Will the Saviour weep, and you will not? We are all 'fearfully and wonderfully made' (Psalm 139:14), and that includes our tear ducts, given in order to be used. Many a child of God in the Bible is found weeping, in addition to Mary over her dead brother, Lazarus: Abraham when he buried his wife, Sarah

(Genesis 23:2); David and Jonathan together (1 Samuel 20:41); Hezekiah before the Lord (2 Kings 20:3); Peter after denying Jesus three times (Luke 22:62); Mary Magdalene at Jesus' tomb (John 20:11). Jeremiah is sometimes known as 'the weeping prophet' (Jeremiah 9:1). Believers' tears have been called 'liquid petitions'. And we find the psalmist David asking God to 'put my tears in your bottle' (Psalm 56:8).

Christians have many reasons to weep. Let me apply this in a personal way.

- Have you never wept over your sins?
- Have you never shed tears of repentance?
- Have you never wept because your heart was breaking (so overwhelmed that you were with sorrow, disappointment or heaviness)?
- Have you never wept alone in secret, even if no one has ever seen you do so?
- Have you never wept over others (a wayward child, a faithless spouse, a friend who has turned against you, an unconverted one)?
- Have you never wept as you have obeyed the biblical injunction to 'weep with those who weep' (Romans 12:15), especially your brothers and sisters in Christ?
- Have you never wept tears of joy at the Lord's mercies to you, his answers to your prayers and his gracious providences in your life?
- Have you never wept and sighed over the state of things in the church, in the nation, in the world, and in the fierce opposition to the gospel?

And this:

- Have you never wept over your lack of progress in holiness (sanctification), and your weak and poor longing for heaven—when, once and for all, 'God will wipe away every tear from [our] eyes' (Revelation 7:17)?
- Have you never wept over the defacing of the beauty of Jesus everywhere around us?

True, some sorrows may be too deep for tears. But may our Christian lives become far less dry-eyed than perhaps they are. 'Jesus wept'; and so may we, if we belong to him and would be like him.

14

Jesus' divine pleasure

John 11:37

There's always one, so the saying goes. Except this time there were several. Verse 37 begins, 'But some of them [the Jews who were among those present] said, "Could not he who opened the eyes of the blind man also have kept this man from dying?"' What a contrast with what some others of them had just said, in the preceding verse, 'See how he [Jesus] loved him [Lazarus]!'

We shall consider their question, recorded in verse 37, in three different ways, in order to explore something of *Jesus' divine pleasure.*

Consider it, first, as a wrong question

The Jews who posed their question here, face to face (as it were) with the Lord Jesus, certainly asked a wrong question. Why? Notably, because they asked it in a wrong spirit. What kind of wrong spirit? A cynical spirit, a malicious spirit; a spirit aimed not at glorifying Jesus and giving him the pre-eminence, but aimed at humiliating him in public, speaking evil of him where others would hear, casting dishonour upon him.

A number of things were built into their question, to make it *a wrong question.*

They found fault with Jesus

Their argument was along these lines: he did this with the blind man (did they have the episode in John 9 in mind?), so why did he not do the same for the sick man, Lazarus? He could have done, so he should have done. The man did not need to die. They were determined to pick holes. They refused to think well of him.

They cast doubt upon Jesus

They cast doubt upon *his love* for the three Bethany siblings. They argued that if Jesus really loved them, would he not have demonstrated that love in preventing Lazarus from dying, and so saving his sisters all this terrible grief?

They cast doubt upon *his wisdom* in the situation. Does he not really know what he is doing? Does he not see what his refusal to act will lead to?

They cast doubt upon *his power*. Was it, perhaps, that he did not act because he could not act? Did he lack the power to do so? Did he lack the necessary authority? If he really is the Messiah, if he truly is the one he claims to be who has come from God, if he has already done various mighty works previously, then surely he could easily have saved Lazarus from dying. They would try the same argument later when Jesus was being crucified: '"… save yourself, and come down now from the cross!" So also the chief priests with the scribes mocked him to one another, saying, "He saved others; he cannot save himself. Let the Christ, the King of Israel, come down now from the cross that we may see and believe."' (Mark 15:30–32.)

They cast doubt upon *his whole character*—his heart, his tears, his word, his compassion, his intentions; indeed, everything about him.

They rounded upon Jesus

They desired to know the reason why Jesus had acted as he had done (or, as they saw it, why he had failed to act). And they did so as if he owed them some explanation which, of course, he did not. They would have him justify himself to them. They forgot that God does not answer to men for his actions, neither is he to be questioned concerning them. It is not for him to give an account. There will always remain those 'secret things [that] belong to the LORD our God' (Deuteronomy 29:29).

At the end of the day, they were wasting their time and their breath. They were spouting mere words. They insisted on talking about things that might have been. Speculating over what might have happened. They were set upon pursuing their own vain reasoning, futile arguments and unbelieving hearts.

It was altogether *a wrong question* as originally asked.

Consider it, second, as a right question

At this point, as you read, you might immediately think to yourself—we have just considered these words as a wrong question, so how can it now suddenly turn into a right question? It cannot be both. But that is where you would be mistaken, for we come now to look at the Jews' question in verse 37 in a different light altogether. Put to one side the malice that made it a wrong question, a question proceeding from

Jesus' enemies. As you do so, you will find that exactly the same question can, in different circumstances, with a different spirit, and coming from Jesus' friends become *a right question*. Indeed not only a right question, but God-glorifying, Christ-exalting, faith-strengthening, prayer-encouraging, in every way a blessed question.

What I mean is this: arguing believingly from one thing that Jesus has done to another, and from what Jesus has done even for me to what he might do for someone else, if it is his divine pleasure to do so. Think it through in the following way, on the basis of the verse 37 question. The argument brought is that since Jesus opened the eyes of a blind man, he could have kept another man from dying. In other words, he has already shown what mighty works he can do. So apply the same argument in different ways. Here are four examples of how to do it.

Apply it to salvation

If Jesus has saved one person (you or me, for example), then he can save other people as well (including those for whose conversion you and I pray). Surely, if it is plain that he has done the one, he is able to do the other also.

Apply it to revival

What the Lord has done in the past, in respect of visiting, reviving and refreshing his church, after she has fallen into dry, lean, fruitless and unfaithful days, he can do again—even now in our present day. Surely, if it is plain that he has done it many times already, he is able to do it many times yet.

Apply it to backsliding

Often the Lord in his grace and mercy has reclaimed the backslider, gone after the wanderer, brought home the penitent, and these are things we desire that he would continue to be pleased to do. Surely, if it is plain that this is what he has done before, he can do again.

Apply it to granting us a closer walk with himself

I do not expect that anyone reading this (I include myself who am writing it) dares to imagine that we know all about the Lord God (Father, Son, Spirit) that there is to know, or that we are in the closest daily walk in which it is possible to be, or that we are as holy as we should be and one day will be. Surely, if it is plain from our reading of past worthies (and our fellowship with some present ones) that he has granted such favours before, he can grant them again for us, in our day.

We can never have too large, too exalted, too longing or too expectant views of what the Lord *can do* or what he *may be pleased to do*. Do you see how, in this way, this same question can be transformed into an eminently *right* question?

Consider it, third, as an unnecessary question

Remember what the question was: 'Could not he who opened the eyes of the blind man also have kept this man from dying?' Could he not? Of course he could! But the thing is, that it was not in this Bethany instance *Jesus' divine pleasure* to do so. In this way, therefore, they were asking *a completely unnecessary question*, one that was quite pointless and fruitless. It did not need to be asked, for Jesus had not determined to do what they were suggesting he should have done. Rather, you recall, he had deliberately waited for two days after receiving the message and then arrived in the village after four days, when Lazarus had died.

The question arises: seeing the Lord could have kept Lazarus alive, why did he choose not to do so? The fact is that Jesus had already given his own answer. He had made clear from the beginning what the overriding factor was to be in this whole episode: the glory of God. 'It is for the glory of God' (verse 4). He will underscore this later in verse 40. 'Did I not tell you that if you believed you would see the glory of God?' This was the reason why Jesus had not stepped in to stop Lazarus dying. It was precisely in order that he might set forth the glory of God, and do so in the most remarkable manner by raising him from the dead, even after he had been in the tomb for four days (note verse 39).

This is always what governs every divine action and every divine pleasure: God's own glory. He is jealous for that glory, and declares, 'I will be jealous for my holy name' (Ezekiel 39:25b). Jealousy, which can be a vice with us, is a virtue (and a glorious virtue) with God. It speaks especially of his concern for his own glory (which he will not share with anyone or anything else) and of his passion for his own people (from whom he desires and requires undivided loyalty and devotion).

Here in John 11 we see clearly several ways in which God was glorified.

He was glorified for Lazarus' sake

What an honour was set upon Lazarus, so to experience the almighty power of God stretched forth on his behalf. Indeed, 'Jesus loved … Lazarus' (verse 5). Indeed, 'See how he loved him!' (verse 36). Lazarus was a true believer before all this happened, yet with what assurance and blessing must the precious things of God have come home to his soul after this amazing experience of affliction and deliverance. It would certainly have been a mighty work if Jesus had 'kept this man from dying'. Yet it was a mightier work by far that Jesus chose to perform by raising him from death!

He was glorified for Mary and Martha's sake

How he loved them, too: 'Now Jesus loved Martha and her sister'. Just think of the joys he brought them and the devotions that these joys will have brought forth from their overflowingly thankful hearts. It will surely have been for their spiritual and practical education and benefit, their profit as a result of which they would both 'grow in the grace and knowledge of [their] Lord and Saviour Jesus Christ' (2 Peter 3:18). What ultimate gainers Martha and Mary must have been by their sore (if brief) trial, in order to witness the glorious outcome. Some of God's promises are (so to speak) written in the sort of invisible ink you hear of which does not show until you hold it to the fire; they can only be read by the firelight of affliction.

He was glorified for the Jews' sake

That applies to the acknowledgers of verse 36 and the moaners of verse 37. In the light of Jesus' miracle, they would both be without excuse. Truly, the Messiah had come among them. Sadly for some, the more they saw of Jesus and the more they heard of him, the harder of heart they grew. Others, happily, were graciously and savingly worked upon. The result in each case is recorded for us in verses 45 and 46: 'Many of the Jews, therefore, who had come with Mary and had seen what he did, believed in him, but some of them went to the Pharisees and told them what Jesus had done.'

The personal response

Do you ask questions? If so, do you ask wrong questions, right questions or unnecessary questions; or, at different times, a combination of all three? The question of verse 37 revolves around response to the Lord Jesus Christ. What is your response to him, to Jesus himself (who he is and what he has done) and to the gospel (good news) of salvation preached in his name? What questions does all this prompt in your mind?

Make a point of steering well away from wrong questions and unnecessary questions. Have no truck with doubting, complaining, accusing, ungrateful questions (which evidence a wrong or proud spirit before the Lord). Avoid questions which suggest that the Lord is, for some reason, obliged to tell you everything, explain all his purposes to you, or give an account of his dealings.

Be sure to ask *the right questions* of the Lord. And what are they?

If you are not yet a Christian, the right questions to ask will include these:

- To whom should I go? Answer: 'Seek the LORD while he may be found; call upon him while he is near' (Isaiah 55:6).
- How should I pray? Answer: 'God, be merciful to me, a sinner!' (Luke 18:13).
- What should I do? Answer: 'Believe in the Lord Jesus, and you will be saved ...' (Acts 16:31).

If you are already a Christian, the right questions to ask include these:

- To whom should I go? Answer: 'Humble yourselves, therefore, under the mighty hand of God so that at the proper time he may exalt you, casting all your anxieties on him, because he cares for you' (1 Peter 5:6–7).

- How should I pray? Answer: 'Lord, "increase [my] faith!"' (Luke 17:5).
- What should I do? Answer: 'Strive for … the holiness without which no one will see the Lord' (Hebrews 12:14).

15

Jesus' triple challenge

John 11:38–41

There is certainly a real-life drama unfolding before us here in this chapter of John's gospel! Now, in these verses, we come to more. We are faced here with *Jesus' triple challenge.*

What was happening here, as we are about to discover, was very much a challenge to Lazarus' sisters, Mary and Martha (although only Martha is mentioned by name and speaks in these verses). And it was a strong challenge as well to all who were gathered there, whatever they thought of Jesus (whether they belonged to the verse 36 or the verse 37 brigades), and whatever they imagined was going to happen.

Consider the triple challenge in this way:

It was a challenge to keener action

One point needs to be insisted upon straightaway. There are many things which God alone can do. They depend entirely and exclusively upon his sovereign power and working. We can have no part in their doing. They ever remain completely outside our sphere of ability or operation, and raising Lazarus from the dead was certainly one of them.

If ever Lazarus was to come out of his tomb alive only a divine act could accomplish it. He could do nothing for himself. His sisters could not help. His friends were impotent. The crowds standing around were useless in the matter. Why so? For the single reason just given: there are many things which God alone can do, and this is one.

There is another point which also requires insisting upon. There are many things which God commands and requires *us* to do. Things which, in humble and dutiful obedience, we must do. Sometimes the commands he lays upon *us* to do turn out to be preparatory for something else which *he* is then going to do. But we must first do as we are told.

An instance of this is now before us. The Lord Jesus is going to do something which only he can do, and we cannot: bring a dead man back to life. Before he does that he gives a clear command to those gathered with him. Jesus had, we are told, come to the tomb where Lazarus had been laid and, we are also told, he was 'deeply moved again' (verse 38—remember verse 33). Now he issued his command to those gathered there: 'Jesus said, "Take away the stone"' (verse 39). He could, of course, have removed the stone himself, but he does not do himself what he would have us do. He does not put forth his power unnecessarily.

Another example of this can be found in John 2, in the well-known incident of the miracle of water into wine at the marriage in Cana. First, the servants were to fill the water jars with water; only then did Jesus perform the miracle. Or there is the business of the fishermen putting out into deep water and letting their nets down again, having not caught a single fish all night. Only when they had obeyed Jesus' command did he provide the miraculous catch of fish in Luke 5. The instance of the healing of the man with the withered hand (Matthew 12) and the miracle with the loaves and fish (Mark 6) provide two further examples. Take a moment to look up these four events and observe the principle we are considering here. Can you think of any other ones where the same applied?

How may this relate to us in our Christian lives? It does so in several ways, of which here are a few examples. Only God can save a sinner; yet we are to be faithful witnesses to unbelievers and faithful preachers of the gospel (2 Timothy 4:2). Only God can regenerate our children and grandchildren; yet we are to do all we can to 'bring them up in the discipline and instruction of the Lord' (Ephesians 6:4). Only God, ultimately, can make us holy and fit us for his presence in heaven; yet it is our business to 'seek the things that are above' (Colossians 3:1), crucifying 'the flesh with its passions and desires' (Galatians 5:24). Only God can revive his church; yet we are to pray earnestly for him to do so, after the manner of the psalmist: 'Will you not revive us again, that your people may rejoice in you?' (Psalm 85:6.)

Absolutely all that we do has to be in total dependence upon the Lord for wisdom, strength and everything else, for apart from him we can do nothing (recall Jesus' words in John 15:5). But the challenging lesson being set before us here, the first part of Jesus' triple challenge, is that while only God can work the works of God (and let us never forget it), yet there are countless occasions when he requires something of us. The call to 'Take away the stone' is one such, and provides a remarkable illustration of the truth that 'we are God's fellow workers' (1 Corinthians 3:9).

Here is the challenge to keener action. Let us be ever ready!

It was a challenge to firmer faith

It is quite clear from the account that Martha was horrified at the thought of the stone being removed, and she does not hesitate to say why: 'Martha, the sister of the dead man, said to him [Jesus], "Lord, by this time there will be an odour [or, 'by this time he stinks'], for he has been dead four days."' The phrase, 'for he has been dead four days', conveys the force of 'a man of four days' or 'a fourth-day man'. It appears that the Jews, by and large, reckoned that by the fourth day after death the body would have become so altered and corrupted that you could not even be sure whose body it was. So Martha says what she says in verse 39, which amounts really to a statement of unbelief. Had she forgotten all that Jesus had said to her earlier (especially in verses 25–26), as well as her own confession of faith in him which followed in verse 27? Strangely, although we know how much she loved her brother, how grieved she was at his death, and (no doubt) how much she would have loved to have him back, she obviously did not like the idea of the stone being moved from the mouth of the cave where Lazarus had been laid.

Here then is the second part of Jesus' triple challenge, calling us to firmer faith. Notice Jesus' immediate response to Martha: 'Jesus said to her, "Did I not tell you that if you believed you would see the glory of God?"' (verse 40). She had neglected to store up Jesus' word in her heart in this matter (Psalm 119:11), the word that he had spoken in his message of verse 4 and in what he said in verse 23. She had forgotten something she needed to remember. She had failed, at this point, to 'Let the word of Christ dwell in [her] richly' (Colossians 3:16). It had stayed on the surface and had not sunk in. She had not taken care to be a doer 'of the word' and not merely a hearer (James 1:22), and so was falling short at a moment when it really mattered. In practical terms, she was not *believing* at this particular moment.

The urgent challenge is set before us to be *believers* in God's word, in every part of it, every detail of it, all of it, all the time. We can be strange characters! One moment, we are full of faith (or imagine that we are), standing on the divine promises, doubting nothing. The next moment, just like dear Martha, down we go. How we need to remember that God's word is the word of 'God, who never lies' (Titus 1:2). Our Lord Jesus will never forget or unsay any word that he has spoken or any promise that he has made. Is that not grand and glorious? No wonder he is called 'Jesus Christ the faithful witness' (Revelation 1:5).

This is something which even the most seasoned or veteran believer needs constant reminding of. We need regularly to hear the words of Jesus to Martha here, 'Did I not tell you?'

It was a challenge to greater expectations

This is the third element in Jesus' triple challenge. Indeed, it is a challenge not merely to *great* expectations but to *even greater* ones. Verse 40 holds the clue: 'you would see the glory of God'.

We mentioned in the previous section that Jesus' raising of Lazarus would bring glory to God in at least three ways: for Lazarus himself, for Mary and Martha, and for the Jews who were present. The thrust of this challenge *to us*, however, is this:

are we (you and I) longing to 'see the glory of God'? It is quite a question. How high are our hopes? How large is our vision? How fervent is our desire? How great are our expectations?

This challenge to greater expectations really arises directly from the previous challenge to firmer faith according to the Scripture principle of 'According to your faith be it done to you' (Matthew 9:29).

At present, 'we walk by faith, not by sight' (2 Corinthians 5:7). We might say that the unbeliever's motto is, 'When I see, I'll believe', but it is a mark of the true believer to say, 'I believe, and I shall see'. Faith precedes sight. That is the regular order, not only in the sense of faith while we are here on earth and sight once we have come to heaven, but also in the sense of faith and sight, believing and seeing all the time while still on earth. And in particular this is true of the glory of God.

How is this so? It is so *in his answering our prayers*, such that God (time and again) answers in a way 'far more abundantly than all that we ask or think' (Ephesians 3:20). It is so *in his causing his excellencies* to shine forth in the Spirit-owned and Spirit-blessed preaching of his word, the scattering (and, on occasions, the converting) of his enemies so that Satan's kingdom is broken down, the preaching of the gospel 'throughout the whole world as a testimony to all nations' (Matthew 24:14), and his taking care of his 'little flock' (Luke 12:32). It is so *in his enabling us* to endure 'to the end' (Mark 13:13), to die well, and to 'come to Zion with singing' (Isaiah 35:10). It is so, and will most certainly prove to be so, *in Jesus' coming again*, when he will 'be marvelled at among all who have believed' (2 Thessalonians 1:10) and 'we will always be with the Lord' (1 Thessalonians 4:17).

How very much we need heavenly grace to enable us, day by day, to stand on the higher ground of greater expectations of the Lord!

Before moving on, however, one more thing needs to be said, and it is very wonderful. Take your thoughts back to Lazarus being 'a four-day man', by which time it was feared that his dead body would be in an unhealthy and odorous condition. Does that suggest anything to you concerning the Lord Jesus? What did Jesus say of himself, prophetically, when addressing his Father in Psalm 16:10? 'For you will not abandon my soul to Sheol [death and the grave], or let your holy one see corruption'. And what did Jesus say about when he would be raised from the dead? It would be 'after three days' (Mark 9:31). Notice that number carefully: 'three'—in the light of which we rejoice to know that our Lord Jesus Christ was *never* a 'fourth-day man'! His body *never* saw 'corruption'. After his death upon the cross (a very real death), he rose from the dead (a very real resurrection) 'on the third day in accordance with the Scriptures' (1 Corinthians 15:4). Which, surely, requires a hearty 'Hallelujah!'.

16

Jesus' prayer life

John 11:41–42

It would be impossible (and certainly incomplete and unbalanced) to attempt to seek a true sight of the Saviour without considering the matter coming now into view: *Jesus' prayer life*. We have in these two verses another intimate cameo portrait, and we stand once again upon holy ground.

Jesus' habit of praying

Unmistakably here we find the Lord Jesus Christ praying. 'And Jesus lifted up his eyes and said …' He then spoke directly to his Father: 'Father, I thank you that you have heard me.' And the hearing is then underscored in this prayer he spoke in public: 'I knew that you always hear me.'

The key thing to note straightaway is that what we encounter Jesus doing here was in no way unusual for him. This moment of prayer (albeit in the hearing of those around him) was not a 'one off', something he was unused to doing. Not at all! It is very much part and parcel of his regular habit of praying, a disciplined priority habit. Indeed, we may say that his was a life of prayer, a prayer life.

Jesus was a man of habit, and not only where prayer was concerned. For example, Luke 4:16 informs us that he was in the habit of going 'to the synagogue on the Sabbath day'. He did so, that verse declares, 'as was his custom'. And as for praying, Luke 5:16 reveals that 'he would withdraw to desolate places and pray'. The well-known verse, Mark 1:35, lets us know that he would do so even 'rising very early in the morning, while it was still dark', when 'he departed and went out to a desolate place, and there he prayed'.

We learn from the gospels that he was praying after his baptism, and it was then that 'the heavens were opened, and the Holy Spirit descended on him … and a voice came from heaven' (Luke 3:21–22). His choice of his twelve apostles followed a whole night of prayer ('all night he continued in prayer to God', Luke 6:12). On the mount of transfiguration, it was 'as he was praying' that 'the appearance of his face was altered, and his clothing became dazzling white' (Luke 9:29). He was praying during his agony in the garden of Gethsemane, during which 'there appeared to him an angel from heaven, strengthening him', as a result of which 'he prayed more earnestly; and his sweat became like great drops of blood falling down to the ground' (Luke 22:41–44). And mark this: he was even praying on the cross, and more than once (see Matthew 27:46 and Luke 23:34 for proof of this).

Furthermore, not only did he pray himself, but he taught about prayer, helped his disciples to pray, and spoke parables about prayer. Would we become more like Jesus? Then let us seek grace to become more like Jesus in this exceedingly vital and practical area—this regular, disciplined, priority habit of prayer. Here is a searching (and exposing?) question for us all if we are Christians. As our Christian lives as a whole have gone on, have our prayer lives in particular gone on also? Where are we, and how are we, in this crucial matter? For it pertains very much to our very *being* if we would be healthy and robust Christians.

If we need a challenge here (and which of us does not?), consider this: If Jesus, the second Person of the Trinity, cherished such a habit of prayer, then how much more should we? If he needed to pray with the constancy he demonstrates, then how much more do we? If he, with his sinless nature, needed to pray, then how much more should we, who were 'brought forth in iniquity' (Psalm 51:5)? If he, on whom 'the ruler of this world' had 'no claim' (John 14:30), prayed, then how much more should we, in whom the devil finds a great deal of cause to bring accusation?

Jesus' intimacy in praying

The intimacy referred to is, of course, his intimacy with the Father. What a great deep we stand on here: the relationship *within the one Godhead* of the *three persons of that same Godhead.* We do well not to say too much. It is not ours to enter into idle (and potentially false) speculation. These matters are too high for us.

Rather, learn from these present verses in John 11 (Jesus' intimacy in prayer) how it reminds us that as a real man Jesus exhibited such affection for his Father, such dependence upon his Father, such obedience to his Father, such a conscious sense or awareness of his Father. All of these things come through loud and clear in his prayer life. We may call it his communion with his Father.

There is such a thing as the school of prayer. We too approach our Father, keeping before us as we do the risen Jesus' words to Mary, when he said, 'I am ascending to my Father and your Father' (John 20:17)—in other words, the same Father! How do we do so? We do so as we come through Jesus himself (pleading his merits, his blood and his righteousness), and in the enabling of the Holy Spirit. Observe how, every time we pray, the entire Godhead is involved. The apostle is very clear about this: 'For through him [Jesus the Son] we both [converted Jews and converted Gentiles] have access in one Spirit to the Father' (Ephesians 2:18).

Right here, in John 11:41, Jesus' first word in prayer is 'Father', and this intimacy continues as his brief prayer proceeds. And while Jesus states in Matthew 11:27 that 'no one knows the Son except the Father, and no one knows the Father except the Son', he goes on (thankfully!) to add the words, 'and anyone to whom the Son chooses to reveal him'.

While in many ways the Son's intimate relationship with the Father was and is unique, even we (who are sinners saved by grace) have been ushered into an intimate relationship with the Father, a key ingredient and expression of which is prayer. What a balm and a refuge it is, therefore, for us as God's children, that 'he has blessed us in the Beloved' (Ephesians 1:6).

Jesus' repose in praying

By repose I would draw attention to the lovely sense of resting, confiding, trusting and enjoying that it captures. We have noticed from earlier verses something of the turmoil of spirit through which Jesus was going (verses 33, 35 and 38). Now, however, that has passed, and all is quiet and in repose.

It is striking that Jesus thanks the Father here for hearing him. We do not have recorded for us the actual words of Jesus' prayer at this point; the implication is that throughout his anguish and weeping he had been praying and directing his soul heavenwards. Now he has the deep inner assurance that he has been heard for his asking. So what does he do? He thanks the Father publicly. And why does he do this? For three reasons: to glorify the Father; to strengthen the faith of the believers present (especially Mary and Martha); and to confront the unbelievers there in the company with the reality of God.

This matter of prayer bringing the blessedness of repose and confidence, for both Jesus and for us who belong to him, is much in view in the Psalms. When we think of the Psalms, we think of the psalmists—they are our brethren who lived the life of faith and prayer before us. But there is far more to the Psalms than the psalmists. Jesus is very much there as well. A few examples will suffice to demonstrate that this is so, in each of which (on one level) the believing psalmist is praying, yet (on a deeper level) the Lord Jesus is praying.

The melancholy beginning of Psalm 13 ('How long, O LORD? Will you forget me for ever? How long will you hide your face from me?'), ends with praise ('I will sing to the LORD, because he has dealt bountifully with me'). The solemn cry with which Psalm 22 commences ('My God, my God, why have you forsaken me?') gives way eventually to the repose of verse 24, when the tempest has past ('he has not hidden his face from him, but has heard, when he cried to him'). The sigh of Psalm 42:7 ('all your breakers and your waves have gone over me'), leads on to the sweet assurance with which this psalm concludes ('Hope in God; for I shall again praise him, my salvation and my God').

Jesus' continuance in praying

The glorious truth to be mined here is this: the praying Lord Jesus Christ of whom we are given such a precious sight here in John 11, praying for his people while he was here on earth, is the very same Lord Jesus Christ whom we have praying for us now that he is in heaven. His praying for us has not ceased, neither will it ever do so. The writer to the Hebrews is explicit here: Jesus, as part of his ongoing ministry as our 'great high priest' (Hebrews 4:14), 'always lives to make intercession for [us]' (Hebrews 7:25). He engages ceaselessly in this praying for all his people, all his disciples, in every age and generation—so that includes us! And just as he gave himself in a 'whole-souled' manner to prayer on earth, holding nothing back, expending great energy, so he prays now. Nothing has abated since 'he sat down at the right hand of the Majesty on high' (Hebrews 1:3). Now, just as much as ever, Jesus, 'who is at the right hand of God … indeed is interceding for us' (Romans 8:34). All that we said about it when dealing with verse 22 of John 11 continues to apply. No change, no weariness.

One more word must be repeated, though, and the heart of it comes directly from the verse presently before us. The Son is always heard by the Father—*always heard*. It is a sheer and absolute impossibility for it ever to be otherwise. He must be heard as he comes for us, prays for us and pleads for us. As regards him in his praying, we have one who 'has entered, not into holy places made with hands, which are copies of the true things, but into heaven itself, now to appear in the presence of God on our behalf' (Hebrew 9:24). On the basis of this, as regards our praying, 'we have confidence to enter the holy places by the blood of Jesus, … since we have a great high priest over the house of God' (Hebrews 10:19, 21).

How very much we owe (maybe, to our shame, without realising it most of the time) to our Lord Jesus' continuance in praying. It is worth repeating: he 'always lives to make intercession for [us]' (Hebrews 7:25)—*always lives*! What more can we ever need than that?

17

Jesus' striking miracle

John 11:43–44

In a sense, everything in this John 11 narrative has been pressing and straining to the point now arrived at, the raising of Lazarus from the dead by the Lord Jesus Christ. Truly we may describe this event as *Jesus' striking miracle.* And *striking* is certainly the word. Moreover, there are two senses in which this is so, two aspects of the matter to be focussed upon. There is the raising of Lazarus himself (that has already happened), and there is the general resurrection coming at the last day (that has yet to happen). This first event is, in some important ways, a foreshadowing of the second. We shall call them *a mighty miracle* and *a mightier miracle.*

A mighty miracle: the raising of Lazarus

This is one of the best known of all Jesus' miracles and stands out as a mighty miracle in a number of ways.

It is mighty even among the other miracles recorded in the gospels where Jesus raises the dead

He raised the dead on other occasions. Think, for example, of the son of the widow of Nain (Luke 7) or the daughter of Jairus (Mark 5). But there is a climactic nature to the raising of Lazarus, a crowning glory to this particular miracle. In the case of the widow of Nain's son, he was dead but had not yet been buried. In that of Jairus' daughter, she had only just died. When it comes to the raising of Lazarus, however, here was a man whose body had been prepared for burial (notice the mention in verse 44 of 'his hands and feet bound with linen strips, and his face wrapped with a cloth'), and had already 'been dead four days' (verse 39).

It is mighty in its demonstration of Jesus as the Lord of life and death

Yet it is remarkable to observe how Jesus' divine power and divine authority was exercised here so simply. We are told that 'he cried out with a loud voice, "Lazarus, come out"'. And that was it; that was all. The very next thing we are told is: 'The man who had died came out'. That verb 'cried out' conveys the sense of a most forcible piercing shout, for all to hear.

The voice of God—what a voice that is! Remind yourself of what is said about it in the series of majestic statements in Psalm 29. At creation, the repeated refrain throughout Genesis 1 is, 'And God said.' Psalm 33:6 declares, 'By the word of the Lord the heavens were made.' It is the same with regeneration, where in 1 Peter 1:23 it is stated, '... since you have been born again, not of perishable seed but of imperishable, through the living and abiding word of God'.

And here with the raising of Lazarus, it is exactly the same.

God speaks, and it is done. He commands, and it takes place. The statement of verse 44 is very emphatic: 'The man who had died came out' is (in the original), 'Came out the one having died [or, the dead man]'. Not just anyone who might have been in the tomb, but *that one,* Lazarus summoned personally. The one who himself is 'the resurrection and the life' (verse 25) here raised Lazarus from the dead, calling him by name out of the tomb, giving him life once again and then adding further, 'Unbind him, and let him go.' And Jesus, he who has 'the keys of Death' (Revelation 1:18), did it *with a word*!

It is mighty in its setting forth the glory of God and the faithfulness of all his promises and ways

There is thus a direct line to be drawn between verse 4 and the present two verses. Remember that Jesus had made plain at the beginning that Lazarus' illness would be 'for the glory of God'. That promise is now fulfilled. As always, 'the word of the LORD proves true' (Psalm 18:30). There are never any exceptions to this, for the Lord is unswervingly faithful in all that he says, and 'never lies' (Titus 1:2).

So for these reasons at least, the raising of Lazarus was unquestionably a mighty miracle. It affords certain proof (if proof were needed) that he is 'the Christ who is God over all, blessed forever' (Romans 9:5).

A mightier miracle: the resurrection at the last day

This takes us back to Jesus' conversation with Martha in verses 23–24, but of necessity makes a return here. Scripture teaches us that God 'has fixed a day on which he will judge the world in righteousness by a man whom he has appointed; and of this he has given assurance to all by raising him from the dead' (Acts

17:31), a reference to Jesus' own resurrection. This day is referred to by Jesus as 'the last day' in a verse like John 6:40: 'For this is the will of my Father, that everyone who looks on the Son and believes in him should have eternal life, and I will raise him up on the last day'. It is equally clear from his words in John 5:28–29 that this day will affect not only believers in Jesus, but all mankind: '… for an hour is coming when all who are in the tombs will hear his voice and come out, those who have done good [believers, with the evidences of true faith and life] to the resurrection of life, and those who have done evil [unbelievers, with no evidences of true faith and life] to the resurrection of judgment.' It will be a universal day, with the entire human race involved and affected with the final judgment.

Much will happen on that day, central to which is Jesus' return 'on the clouds of heaven with power and great glory' (Matthew 24:30), according to Scripture promise. And at this last day there will be this great and general resurrection, or raising of the dead, the very thing which is foreshadowed here in John 11. Yet while the raising of Lazarus is undoubtedly *a mighty miracle*, this resurrection at the last day will be *a mightier miracle* still, and that in at least three ways.

Because of who will be raised from the dead

In John 11, one man is raised. At the end of this 'present evil age' (Galatians 1:4), everyone who has ever lived will be raised. It will be an utterly momentous occasion. On that day, the graves will give up their dead (and it makes no difference how or where people died). The verses from John 5, moreover, stress the going forth and the hearing of the divine 'voice', just as the divine voice was issued in the case of Lazarus. At the sound of this voice, all must obey and all must arise.

What an assembling it will be. The entire population of the world is large enough at most given points in history, but here we are dealing with the entire population that has lived at any and all points in history. Even the company of believers on that day will comprise 'a great multitude that no one could number, from every nation, from all tribes and peoples and languages' (Revelation 7:9): and that is only the believers, before everyone else is counted in! How can you count the countless or number the innumerable? Yet everyone will be there, everyone who has ever lived, from Adam and Eve onwards. As for those who are still alive on the earth at this time (as some inevitably will be), they will be there as well. No one will be missing. You can stay off work, you can be absent from school, you may refuse to go to church, you may turn down all sorts of invitations in life, but you (and I) will be standing there in our appointed place on this day. 'For we must all appear before the judgment seat of Christ' (2 Corinthians 5:10).

Because of the final and eternal nature of the resurrection day

In no way should we minimise or underplay the mightiness of Jesus' miracle in raising Lazarus from the dead. It was a stupendous miracle of divine power. Yet Lazarus was returned to his sisters for a further season of their lives together at Bethany. In a sense, he took things up where he had left them off when he died, but it was only for him to have to die again in due course, and himself be among those present along with the rest of us at the general resurrection at the last day.

In contrast, the resurrection at the last day will have a finality about it, an eternal dimension. Jesus' parable about the sheep and the goats affirms this, with the separation of the sheep (believers, placed on his right hand) and the goats (unbelievers, placed on his left hand). To the former, he will speak these words: 'Come, you who are blessed by my Father, inherit the kingdom prepared for you from the foundation of the world' (Matthew 25:34). To the latter, he will speak these words: 'Depart from me, you cursed, into the eternal fire prepared for the devil and his angels' (Matthew 25:41). And this parable concludes with Jesus saying (speaking now of unbelievers first and then believers), 'And these will go away into eternal punishment, but the righteous into eternal life' (Matthew 25:46). And in light of what we have already observed (and stressed), we cannot help noticing again the divine 'voice' as being central to all of this,

If we have lived saved, we shall rise saved; if we have lived holy, we shall rise holy. If, however, we have lived unbelieving, we shall rise unbelieving; if we have lived Christless, we shall rise Christless. There will be no intervening state of 'purgatory' in order to allow for self-improvement, or room for any other man-made falsehood.

When a believer dies, he or she is immediately in the presence of Jesus, even while the body remains in the earth. When an unbeliever dies, he or she is immediately beyond all possibility of the grace, salvation and blessing to be found alone in the Lord Jesus Christ. Then, at this general resurrection on the last day, all will rise and receive their final assessment from Jesus, seated upon his glorious throne.

Because of the new resurrection bodies which believers will receive on that day

The key Bible passage upon this is 1 Corinthians 15:35–57, a passage which begins with the dual questions: "How are the dead raised? With what kind of body do they come?" It would be worthwhile reading those verses at this point.

When Lazarus was commanded by Jesus to come out of the tomb, and he came out, he did so with precisely the same body with which he had lived previously in Bethany and which had been laid in the tomb. Those who performed Jesus' instructions in verse 44 would soon have discovered this for themselves.

But what of the bodies of believers on the last day? This is where those 1 Corinthians 15 verses are so instructive, with the illustration of sowing and raising—the contrast worked out there between dishonour and glory, weakness and power, natural and spiritual. When we rise from the dead, we shall have left behind us in the grave all the 'grave clothes' of our earthly bodies. Beyond this, however, we cannot go. We must wait and see. Patience and trust are required. It is not spelled out for us, for example, what the mysterious connections might be between our present bodies and our resurrection ones. Where the Bible is silent, let us not be vocal.

Let us end this section on the note, again, of the voice of God. Are you familiar with it? Would you recognise it if you heard it? For be sure, you will most certainly hear it—we all shall. It is a voice which can speak more tenderly than any other voice. It can also speak more awesomely than any other voice. It will be much better to hear it *now* than to turn a deaf ear to it, only to hear it *then* for the first time. For be assured that how ever much or stubbornly you refuse to hear God's voice now, you will most certainly hear it then. As for now—while there is still time for you to do so—this voice calls to you, saying, 'Turn to me and be saved … For I am God, and there is no other' (Isaiah 45:22).

18

Jesus' dividing effect

John 11:45–46

While some people always claim to have no interest whatsoever in the Lord Jesus Christ and carry on as if he did not exist, the deeper truth is that he invariably provokes reactions. That is what is in mind in calling this section *Jesus' dividing effect.* You can see it straightaway, the moment you read these two verses in John 11. Jesus has just raised Lazarus from the dead, and the very next thing we read is this: 'Many of the Jews therefore, who had come with Mary and had seen what he did, believed in him, but some of them went to the Pharisees and told them what Jesus had done.'

Some believed in Jesus, and some did not. Some went one way, and some went another. Some were for him, and some were against him. The point is clear, that Jesus had a dividing effect upon the people gathered there. There is no implication that some reserved their position; no sense at all that some just were not bothered one way or the other. Exactly the opposite—there was a stark and fundamental division over Jesus.

This, of course, should not surprise us, for this is how it has always been and how it continues to be. Taking a 'non-position' about Jesus is never really an option (did you think it was?). Not to be decided *for* him is to be decided *against* him. Dear reader: on which side of the fence are you in this matter? In reality, there is no fence there for you to sit on.

Note carefully each of these two verses: In verse 45 we are given the happy news that 'Many … believed in him'. Even if we allow for the possibility that with some this 'believing' was merely of the moment, was not real and did not last (just like some of the categories in Jesus' parable of the sower, and which, sadly, is the case with some 'professions' of faith in Jesus), yet we should still give full value to the word 'many'. Just think of it: here are these Jewish folk who have seen a mighty work of God performed before their very eyes, and what happened to them? They 'believed in him'. They believed upon Jesus as their Saviour and Lord. They were added to his people on that remarkable day that they would never forget, and they followed him. How wonderful it is whenever that happens, and it still does!

But there is always one (as the familiar saying goes), and on this occasion there were several. Verse 46 begins with the (in context) rather looming word, 'but'. But what? We are told that 'some of them went to the Pharisees'. What did they do that for? What was their game? They did what they did, not only to report the miracle, still less to seek to persuade the authorities to favour Jesus, but rather (as the following verses bear witness) to turn the authorities further against Jesus. And it appears that they did this deliberately and spitefully.

Both companies of people in these two verses had witnessed the same miracle. Both had heard the words of command that

Jesus had spoken, and were fully aware of how those words had immediately been obeyed. But what very different effects everything had upon them. Some were drawn to Jesus, and some were driven from him. Some were softened, and some were hardened. Some believed and some refused to believe. Some publicly gave God the glory, and some conspicuously did not. Again, as it was then, so it is now. The encouragement here, however, is that those who believed were 'many', while those who opposed were 'some'.

This needs our closer investigation.

The effect Jesus has upon people

There is nothing in the least novel in our day about Jesus' dividing effect. That lovely aged pilgrim, Simeon, foretold it in Luke 2:34–35. The apostle Peter confirmed it in 1 Peter 2:6–8. The apostle Paul asserted it in 2 Corinthians 2:15–16. And the dying thief demonstrated it in Luke 23:39–43. Take a well-spent moment to look up each of those verses right now, so that the point sinks well in. And remember, it is always the same!

This is a vital and practical truth: wherever and whenever the Lord Jesus Christ comes into contact with anyone—every time he is spoken of, every time his claims are set forth, every time the true gospel is proclaimed—Jesus *always* has an effect, and that effect is invariably a *dividing* one. It cannot really be otherwise. He is never without influence. He necessarily requires, and indeed, demands a response. Have you not observed (including in your own life) how the very mention of his name can quickly get people going one way or another? The most weighty things can follow when he is even just touched upon, even if it is not apparent straightaway. It can resemble the lighting of the blue touch paper and the need to stand well back!

None of us can ever hear of the Lord Jesus Christ and be the same afterwards as we were before. You cannot be indifferent to him. You respond *for* him or *against* him. You cannot remain neutral or uncommitted (and will most certainly not be so on the day of judgment). There are no 'hands off' experiences where God and the things of God are concerned.

Did you pause a moment ago to check out those verses? If not, please do so now. Remembering the words of Simeon, Jesus is 'appointed for' your 'falling' or 'rising'. Remembering the words of Peter, Jesus is, 'A stone of stumbling, and a rock of offence', or else he is 'a cornerstone chosen and precious, and whoever believes in him will not be put to shame'. Remembering the words of Paul, Jesus is to you 'a fragrance from death to death' or 'a fragrance from life to life'. And remembering the words of the dying thief, you will look believingly *to* Jesus or you will turn rejectingly *from* him.

Just reflect upon what a solemn position this puts you in right now, as you read these words I am writing. They meet you with you being a Christian or with you not being a Christian. This passage of Scripture brings you face to face with the Lord Jesus Christ, maybe not for the first time. It presses this inescapable question upon you: what are you going to do with Jesus? 'What do you think about the Christ?' (Matthew 22:42), a question which Jesus himself asked on that occasion. He is bound to have some effect upon you. It cannot be otherwise. Which effect is it going to be?

The effect Jesus had upon many

Look again at verse 45, where we are told that those who believed in Jesus numbered 'many'. This prompts a most important question for us all. Who are such, those who believe upon Jesus? What are they like? What characteristics do they display?

They are hungry souls who long to be filled, sinful souls who long to be cleansed, naked souls who long to be clothed, helpless souls who long to be rescued, fallen souls who long to be raised, wretched souls who long to be forgiven, burdened souls who long to be relieved, empty souls who long to be supplied, thirsty souls who long to be satisfied. How? By and through the Lord Jesus Christ, and him alone.

Is that you or me? Of one thing we may be assured, writer and reader alike. All who are among such, to them Jesus' gracious gospel invitation comes in all its fulness of tenderness and power: 'Come to me, all who labour and are heavy laden, and I will give you rest' (Matthew 11:28). He is the mighty God-Man, who raised Lazarus from the dead, and who 'came into the world to save sinners' (1 Timothy 1:15), went to the cross 'that he might bring us to God' (1 Peter 3:18), and himself rose from the dead, 'the living one' who declares 'I am alive forevermore' and has 'the keys of Death and Hades' (Revelation 1:18). And whoever looks to him, calls on him, trusts in him, leans on him, abandons every other refuge apart from him, and comes sorrowing and repenting over their sin—all such will be accepted, forgiven, saved and reconciled to God. How amazingly *free* the gospel offer is. 'Everyone who calls on the name of the Lord will be saved' (Romans 10:13). Surely all such are the most blessed people on the face of the earth!

The effect Jesus had upon some

Look again at verse 46, where we are told that those who did not believe in Jesus numbered 'some'. And verses 53 and 57, when we come to them, will reveal what their refusing to believe led to. The really solemn thing is that just like the others (the ones who believed in Jesus), this company will have come to comfort Mary and Martha, they will have beheld Jesus' agonies, seen his tears, and heard his mighty voice as it awoke the dead man; they will even have heard him thanking and praising God. Yet the effect upon them was so completely and utterly different!

So this prompts another most important question for us all. Who are such, those who do not believe in Jesus? What are they like? What characteristics do they display?

They are proud souls who refuse to be humbled, unbelieving souls who refuse to be persuaded, self-righteous souls who refuse to be exposed, 'wise' souls who refuse to be taught, 'religious' souls who refuse to be challenged, tough souls who refuse to be pricked, satisfied souls who refuse to be blessed, sinful souls who refuse to be saved. And how would these transformations that they will have nothing of take place? By and through the Lord Jesus Christ, and him alone.

Is that you or me? Of another thing we may be assured, writer and reader alike. All who are among such, then the only other option to having the Lord Jesus as your gracious, wonderful and eternal Saviour—the *only* other option—is to face him as your righteous and eternal Judge. Listen even now, as you read them again, to the glorious words of Jesus back in verses 25–26, which concluded with his challenging and highly personal question: 'Do you believe this?' And remember

Martha's reply: 'Yes, Lord.' Jesus, who raised Lazarus from the dead, is the only one who raises dead sinners to spiritual life. Nothing and no one else can ever save you. Jesus is the one! And if you have not done so already, now is the time to ask him!

19

Jesus' precious death

John 11:47–57

Have you ever said anything, only to discover (maybe much later on) a far deeper significance to your words than ever occurred to you at the time? Or perhaps you have said something at some time, and you are still completely unaware of the far deeper significance of your words. Well, as we now approach the final part of this marvellous chapter of the Bible, John 11, we have a classic instance of someone saying something, yet not really having a clue about the deeper significance of his words.

The plot thickens here. Within this passage, our special focus is upon the words spoken of Jesus by Caiaphas, the high priest, words which bear very directly upon *Jesus' precious death*. We noticed in verses 45–46 the dividing effect which the Lord Jesus had upon the people, many being for him and some being against him. Sadly, some in that second category hated Jesus so much that they 'went to the Pharisees and told them what Jesus had done'. The Pharisees were some of Jesus' deadliest enemies. This move on their part led to schemes to murder Jesus. 'So from that day on they made plans to put him to death' (verse 53). Oh! the desperate wickedness in the hearts of sinners. Oh! the ignorance in which Jesus' enemies reason and the folly in which they act. It was always so, and it continues to be so throughout this present age, until Jesus returns as he has promised to do.

Upon the reports of these haters of Jesus, a meeting was convened. 'So the chief priests and the Pharisees gathered the Council and said, "What are we to do?"' The ultimate upshot of this was that they 'killed the Author of life' (Acts 3:15), they 'crucified the Lord of glory' (1 Corinthians 2:8). The authorities were terrified. 'For this man performs many signs. If we let him go on like this, everyone will believe in him, and the Romans will come and take away both our place and our nation.' They were not interested in right and justice but were only in it for themselves, to save their own skins.

So Caiaphas intervened, and it is verses 49–53 which provide our focus. These few but critical verses record what the high priest said (verses 49–50), followed by John's explanatory comment (verses 51–53). Both are deeply instructive for us. Pay close attention.

I mentioned in beginning this section the business of not realising the significance of words we speak. This is precisely what is happening here. In saying, '... it is better for you that one man should die for the people, not that the whole nation should perish', all Caiaphas *thought* he was saying was this: the best thing to do in the circumstances is to get rid of Jesus, put him out of the way—in other words, kill him. Better that, he argued (one man perishing), than that the entire nation perish (at the hand of the Romans). That is what he said and

I am sure that is all he imagined he was saying. But amazingly, wonderfully, his words had hidden depths. Observe what we are told: 'He did not say this of his own accord [literally, 'from himself'], but being high priest that year he prophesied …' We may dare to express it this way: the Holy Spirit was obliging Caiaphas to use words which take us to the very heart of the gospel. How so? In this way: he utters (unwittingly) a prediction that Jesus' death will bring life to a lost world. And so it did and so it still does! Even more particularly, Caiaphas lays out (never realising that he was doing so) the *central gospel doctrine of substitution* (one person dying in the place of another).

Leaving Caiaphas behind, therefore (where he is best left), and being taken up now only with Jesus, our final *sight of the Saviour* focuses upon his unique death, and this matter of substitution.

The background of substitution

This great truth of Jesus' death being substitutionary has a richly seamed Old Testament background. Three of the leading instances of this are the Passover lamb (Exodus 12), the scapegoat (Leviticus 16), and the suffering Servant (Isaiah 53).

First, *the Passover lamb*. At the first Passover, immediately prior to the divine deliverance of the Jews from their oppression in Egypt under Pharaoh, their being spared from the judgment of God which came upon the Egyptians was secured by means of the substitutionary death of a lamb. When we come to the New Testament, we discover how Jesus' death is the fulfilment of the Passover lamb. He suffered and died *in the place of* his people. His life was laid down, his sacrifice of himself was offered on the cross, his blood was shed, the judgment our sins deserve was laid upon him. 'For Christ, our Passover lamb, has been sacrificed' (1 Corinthians 5:7). We have been 'ransomed from the futile ways inherited from [our] forefathers, not with perishable things such as silver or gold, but with the precious blood of Christ, like that of a lamb without blemish or spot' (1 Peter 1:18–19).

Second, *the scapegoat.* 'And Aaron shall lay both his hands on the head of the live goat, and confess over it all the iniquities of the people of Israel, and all their transgressions, all their sins' (Leviticus 16:21a). He then sent it away into the wilderness to die. The 'scapegoat' is depicted as bearing our sin, guilt and punishment, being condemned to death in our place. This is what has happened in the Lord Jesus. It is a 'picture' of what happened at Calvary. 'So Jesus also suffered outside the gate in order to sanctify the people through his own blood' (Hebrews 13: 12). 'There is therefore now no condemnation for those who are in Christ Jesus' (Romans 8:1).

Third, *the suffering servant.* Substitution lies so obviously at the heart of Isaiah 53, and it is very significant that this chapter is quoted seven times in the New Testament, in direct connection with the person and work of the Lord Jesus Christ, including that beautiful incident in the Acts of the Apostles of the conversion of the Ethiopian eunuch. After Isaiah 53:7–8 is quoted there, the narrative continues in this way: 'And the eunuch said to Philip, "About whom, I ask you, does the prophet say this, about himself or about someone else?" Then Philip opened his mouth, and beginning with this Scripture he told him the good news about Jesus.' (Acts 8:34–35.)

The bearing of substitution

What was Jesus 'bearing' as the sinner's substitute?

He was bearing our sins

'To him all the prophets bear witness that everyone who believes in him receives forgiveness of sins through his name' (Acts 10:43). On the cross, the sins of the sinful ones were being charged to the sinless one. The chief thing which makes sin so very serious is that it is against God. This came home forcibly to David, as he expresses himself in Psalm 51: 'For I know my transgressions, and my sin is ever before me. Against you, you only, have I sinned and done what is evil in your sight, so that you may be justified in your words and blameless in your judgment.' (verses 3–4.). And this provision of our forgiveness cost Jesus nothing less than his own life. 'He himself bore our sins in his body on the tree, that we might die to sin and live to righteousness' (1 Peter 2:24). There at Calvary, Jesus 'suffered once for sins, the righteous for the unrighteous, that he might bring us to God' (1 Peter 3:18). *He* died that *we* can be forgiven.

He was bearing God's wrath

It is not merely that God *detests* sin. He must actually *punish* sin by pouring out his wrath and his anger upon it. What the Lord Jesus does in dying as our substitute is not to cancel God's wrath but to receive its full outpouring upon himself. It has been diverted from us to him. He is 'Jesus who delivers us from the wrath to come' (1 Thessalonians 1:10). This, not least, is what explains the 'darkness over all the land [or, earth]', and Jesus' cry from the cross, 'My God, my God, why have you forsaken me?' (Matthew 27:45–46). In those solemn and dark hours, Jesus was enduring the wrath of God, the wrath of his own Father, 'who did not spare his own Son but gave him up for us all' (Romans 8:32).

He was bearing sin's separation

Consider again those two verses from Matthew's gospel just quoted. Because God is holy, just and true, and because sin is vile, offensive and separating, we must ask where that leaves us sinners? Precisely in this position, where God declares, 'your iniquities [one of the family of Bible words for sins] have made a separation between you and your God, and your sins have hidden his face from you' (Isaiah 59:2). 'God is light, and in him is no darkness at all' (1 John 1:5). He is 'of purer eyes than to see evil and cannot look at wrong' (Habakkuk 1:13). So in standing in our place, as our substitute, what did God's beloved Son in whom is all his delight have to bear? Separation from the Father. It is utterly beyond us to comprehend what that felt like for Jesus. What a black moment, what a terrible curse, what a solemn experience. We dare not say more.

The blessings of substitution

The apostle Paul announces that God 'has blessed us in Christ with every spiritual blessing in the heavenly places' (Ephesians 1:3), some of which are then listed (such as redemption, forgiveness, adoption and the sealing of the Holy Spirit). In Colossians 2:10 Paul makes another grand announcement: we 'have been filled in him [Jesus]'. Perhaps most exquisitely of all, we are told in John 1:16 that 'from his [Jesus'] fullness we have all received, grace upon grace'.

We are graciously favoured and blessed with the complete removal of the penalty which had been written large against us, the complete taking away of our sins which lay heavily upon us, and the complete satisfaction of the Father in his acceptance of all that the Son has done for us.

Here are two further expressions of these mighty truths:

'And you, who were dead in your trespasses …, God made alive together with him [Jesus], having forgiven us all our trespasses, by cancelling the record of debt that stood against us with its legal demands. This he set aside, nailing it to the cross.' (Colossians 2:13–14.) Although '… while we were enemies we were reconciled to God by the death of his Son' (Romans 5:10).

All of this is God's doing, God's gift. *He* took all the steps we could never take to satisfy his own justice and to remove his own judgment. *He* sent his own Son to suffer and die in our place. And going back to the words Caiaphas spoke (without him realising just what he was saying), it is of God's own design and pleasure that Jesus (by his death and, with it, his resurrection, which is the seal of the Father's acceptance of and pleasure in his death) is able 'also to gather into one the children of God who are scattered abroad' (John 11:52). And through it all, Jesus is crowned with glory and honour!

To finish with

We have been taking together *A Sight of the Saviour*. So far as this book is concerned, this sight has concluded. In reality, however, it has only just begun. I mentioned, as we began, that we see more and appreciate more of some sights the more we look at them. That, surely, is true of a sight of the Lord Jesus Christ. We have touched here upon nineteen aspects of his person and work, yet there is still so much more to say and so much more to see. But we have made a start, and I hope very much that you have found it helpful and appetizing!

Whatever your spiritual condition, Christian or not yet so, let me encourage you in two related directions. The first is this: be regular, disciplined and hungry in reading the Bible. Here is food and blessing awaiting you. Here you will see Jesus, time after time. The second is this: wherever in the Bible you are reading at any time (and it is a big book!), make it a priority to read frequently and repeatedly from the four gospels (Matthew, Mark, Luke and John). The reason for this is simple: it is so vital to keep a sight of the Saviour before you all the time. You cannot see too much of him and it is the blessed and promised ministry of God the Holy Spirit to help you. For, says Jesus, concerning this work of the Spirit: 'He will glorify me, for he will take what is mine and declare it to you' (John 16:14).

On one occasion during his ministry, some people approached one of Jesus' disciples with this straight to the point request: 'Sir, we wish to see Jesus' (John 12:21). May that same request always be ours, and may the Lord be pleased to favour us abundantly in his response, so that, constantly and ever more expansively, we are given *A Sight of the Saviour*!

DANE ORTLUND
SURPRISED
by
JESUS
Subversive Grace in the Four Gospels